THE MODERATOR'S HANDBOOK

THE MODERATOR'S HANDBOOK

A Comprehensive Guide for Facilitating Panels

KATRINA DUDLEY

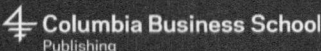

Columbia University Press
Publishers Since 1893
New York   Chichester, West Sussex

Copyright © 2025 Columbia University Press
All rights reserved

Library of Congress Cataloging-in-Publication Data
Names: Dudley, Katrina author
Title: The moderator's handbook : a comprehensive guide for
facilitating panels / by Katrina Dudley.
Description: New York : Columbia University Press, [2025] |
Includes index.
Identifiers: LCCN 2025015380 | ISBN 9780231215084 hardback |
ISBN 9780231222495 trade paperback | ISBN 9780231560610 ebook
Subjects: LCSH: Forums (Discussion and debate)
Classification: LCC LC6519 .D78 2025 |
DDC 371.3/7—dc23/eng/20250530

Cover design: Noah Arlow
Cover image: Shutterstock

GPSR Authorized Representative: Easy Access System Europe,
Mustamäe tee 50, 10621 Tallinn, Estonia

CONTENTS

Foreword by Ranji Nagaswami   vii
Acknowledgments   xi

Introduction   1
1 Why You Need a Panel How-To Guide   8
2 What Is a Moderator?   18
3 Before You Accept the Assignment   31
4 Prepanel Planning   42
5 Selecting Panelists   53
6 Panel Structure and Logistics   67
7 Panelist Preparation Calls   81
8 Marketing the Panel   94
9 Preparing Your Questions   101
10 Opening Speeches and Panelist Introductions   117
11 Speaker Brief   124
12 Advice for Panelists   131
13 Advice for Organizers   142

14 Prepanel Day Pep Talk   147

15 The Day of the Panel   159

16 Onstage Advice   169

17 Handling Audience Questions   180

18 Panel Hiccups   189

19 After the Event   199

Index   207

FOREWORD

Much is written about the skills leaders in business and society, as changemakers, need to succeed. Far less is available to those seeking to change and influence these changemakers—the instigators, provocateurs, and questioners; the "moderators" who, by their questions, empathy, firmness of communication, and training, can move groups and leaders to engage in dialogue and self-work to create desirable outcomes.

My first experience with skilled moderators was as a Henry Crown Fellow at the Aspen Institute, the U.S.-based nonprofit whose founding purpose is to ignite human potential to build understanding and create new possibilities for a better world. Like all fellows in the institute's global leadership programs, I participated in seminars led by moderators carefully selected and trained in the world-renowned "Aspen Socratic Method" of values-based dialogue. Aspen moderators guide provocative, respectful, and sometimes uncomfortable discussions to open minds and hearts and move leaders "from success to significance."

For over a decade, I have now trained moderators and led discussions and seminars myself as an Aspen Institute moderator and founder of the Finance Leaders Fellowship (FLF) program there. My co-moderators and I nudge the fellows—successful leaders across the global finance industry—to consider their roles and their values as leaders in finance and to use their platform and success to advance the role of finance. Throughout the program, fellows interact with one another, debate key topics, and explore ways to become enlightened leaders and deepen their impact. Done right, thoughtful moderating stimulates deep inner explorations and vulnerability with a view to igniting action and societal impact.

When Katrina interviewed for the FLF program, as much as I was interested in asking her questions about her life's work and mission, we quickly found ourselves in a deep discussion about the moderating aspects of the seminar, the Aspen discussion format, moderator training methods, and what makes a successful moderator. On my distilling some of the key Aspen Institute disciplines of effective moderating, such as "getting the talkers to listen and the listeners to talk" and knowing "how to read the room" to understand how hard or delicately to push a particular point, Katrina was intrigued.

Prepared and skilled moderators play a critical yet somewhat invisible (if done right) role in any program's success. Moderators start by understanding who is in the room—each participant's background and what they bring to the dialogue. We use thoughtful questions that build on each other and on the discussion among the group to identify the mosaic of different views and experiences that will join the group in common conversation and purpose. In my experience, the most successful discussions are those where the participants transcend themselves, are taken to a new plateau, and realize they can achieve more.

Confident humility is a moderator's most important trait. For a moderator to succeed, the panelists or discussion participants must be at the forefront, with the humble moderator ever-present but rather invisible in the background. Yet the moderator's confidence is needed to provoke, redirect, and create energy in the discussion. Handling controversy is another key trait of a skilled moderator; addressing and discussing variant perspectives enlightens the entire room. A successful moderator can move beyond the gibberish and the superficial and have deeply penetrating discussions addressing key issues meaningfully. Whether moderating a fellow seminar at the Aspen Institute or a panel at an off-site meeting or conference, moderating is a learned skill. The audience becomes the winner when the moderator can weave the multiple threads of a discussion carefully and press panelists for original thought. The audience will leave the panel presentation having learned something new and exciting.

Like most personal and professional growth paths, a good teacher and preparation are invaluable to help you in the journey. In the pages of Katrina's how-to guide, you will learn from expert moderators who have shared their advice throughout. You will also begin to develop your own toolbox of ways to keep a panel moving, get a panelist back on topic, or handle a disruptive audience, which will develop your confidence. This book provides the training and guidance that you need to become an experienced and successful moderator. In my opinion, it is much needed in a world where skilled moderators asking the right questions of leaders and doers can inspire the latter groups to better themselves and the world around them. Katrina has shared her toolkit, and I think you will benefit from her many years of experience.

I wish you happy reading and welcome you to the joys of mastering your moderator craft.

—Ranji Nagaswami
Finance Industry Leader
Chief Executive and Chief Investment Officer
of leading global asset management firms
Chief Investment Advisor to Mayor Michael Bloomberg

ACKNOWLEDGMENTS

Many years ago, the prime brokerage department of a prominent investment bank asked me to moderate a panel at one of their signature conferences. It was a discussion between five hedge fund managers and me. The panel organizers made a few suggestions, including holding individual calls with each panelist, having a group call, and requesting copies of published shareholder letters. During that experience I learned the importance of thoughtful preparation and as I stood on-stage moderating the discussion, the benefits of preparation helped me negotiate some potentially tricky situations seamlessly. When I was asked to return the following year to moderate a similar panel, I asked the organizers why: my energy and confidence, the positive responses from the audience, and the feedback they had received from the panelists who felt they had been given a fair opportunity to share their experience and views.

The panel was the first of many. Over time, I have further developed my moderator skills through observing others (both good and bad) and speaking with other professionals. One question that I have asked good moderators is whether they have received training. Most have said no but that they wished there had been a guide, like the one provided in this book, to help them on their journey.

There are many people to thank for their help throughout this process. First, I would like to thank my many interviewees. This book would not be as robust as it is without the support of the many moderators I interviewed and quoted throughout this book and a few additional people interviewed off the record. I thank all of them for taking the time to speak with me and share their advice and tips for becoming an influential moderator.

Aspen fellow Ranji Nagaswami inspired me to continue developing the idea of a how-to guide to moderating panels. Our discussions about the important role a moderator plays in many Aspen Institute forums helped shape this book and its content. I am grateful to her thoughtful comments and contributions.

Myles C. Thompson, my editor at Columbia University Press, encouraged me to write and publish this book, and I thank him and his colleague Brian Smith for their support. Thank you to Catherine Chisnall for your input and editorial talents.

My family, Sarah, Emma, Christopher, William, our dogs Bondi and Sydney, and my husband, Todd Jacobson, were with me throughout this journey. I cannot thank them enough for their support during the long days and nights I was writing and editing.

THE MODERATOR'S
HANDBOOK

INTRODUCTION

The Holy Grail—a fun, informative conversation and idea exchange in service of the audience.
—Deirdre Bolton, Head of Executive Development, Prosek Partners

Have you ever sat in the audience of a panel composed of impressive thought leaders and walked away completely underwhelmed?

People often complain about dull, lifeless, and confusing panels. Despite the presence of qualified experts, the panel doesn't advance thought on the topic. While experts share their opinions, their expertise is disguised by a series of moderator mistakes that could be easily prevented. Moderators with ill-considered questions, irrelevant introductions, and disordered content all have the same impact—devaluing the panel. The result of a poorly organized and structured panel discussion is that audience members, panelists, and conference organizers walk away wishing they could regain the time they just gave to the panel discussion.

An engaged, energetic, and well-prepared moderator can solve this problem.

Being a moderator is a great job. It can help advance your career professionally, hone your leadership skills, and showcase your ability to bring out the best in others. Yet despite all these benefits, only some people believe or are aware that you need to prepare for the role to successfully navigate the opportunity. When asked to moderate a panel, some moderators just "wing it." Other moderators might do a brief online search and get tips from the "experts." Ultimately, they need a comprehensive, start-to-finish guide on how to do the job well. They need someone to guide them through the process so they can become the best moderator possible. A step-by-step process on how to moderate panels can make the moderator's role more fulfilling, enjoyable, and successful.

> I enjoy moderating panels because I almost always meet new personalities and get the opportunity to ask people questions that I typically don't get to ask.
> —JEREMY KOHOMBAN, PHD, PRESIDENT AND CEO, THE CHILDREN'S VILLAGE, AND PRESIDENT, HARLEM DOWLING

The goal of a panel is to effectively convey information to an audience. Panels frequently occur at conferences, lunch presentations, and industry events. They are interactive formats where a moderator makes a statement and poses a question, which is then answered by one or more panelists. Each panelist is allotted time to answer the questions and provide the audience with the information.

A panel should not be a series of separate and disconnected monologues. To be successful, it must flow seamlessly from panelist to panelist, unifying multiple experts' opinions, perspectives, and experiences around a common theme or purpose.

The primary purpose and goal of every panel should be centered on the desire to have a discussion that benefits the audience. A talented moderator has an important role to play. They will be able to seamlessly mold the views of diverse experts into a comprehensive and cohesive discussion focused on a shared vision. If successful, an effective moderator will orchestrate an event where the audience leaves the room having learned something new or intriguing and that they want to share with others, and the panelists feel as though they have participated in a discussion where meaningful and impactful insights were shared.

> People and ideas are at the center of it, and I think panels provide spaces where we can discover those ideas and unlock them and almost in a way, workshop them in a public setting, or even private setting, where you have an audience and a lot of energy in the room.
> —NICOLE VALENTINE, FINTECH DIRECTOR, MILKEN INSTITUTE

Panelists engage with the moderator and sometimes will even engage with each other. "Knowing the panelists, doing the work, and being prepared" is how one frequent moderator describes the experience.

A successful moderator ensures each of the panelists is given a chance to shine. After all, panelists are lending their time to this endeavor. A good panel is lively but not disorganized or chaotic. A good moderator with a well-prepared event outline, engaging questions, and a topic of interest should give your panel all the essential ingredients needed for a successful event.

An ineffective moderator doesn't use this power wisely, which can have disastrous consequences. It can lead to a completely chaotic panel. A poor moderator will not direct the questions equitably across the panelists—the questions are "thrown out there" with the expectation that one of the panelists will respond. The risk the moderator faces is that one panelist dominates the discussion to the detriment of other panelists. If they don't cut the dominant panelist off or reduce the speaking time of the other panelists, the panel may go over the allotted time. This is unfair to the next panel that might get shortened. Finally, it is not just verbose panelists the moderator has to monitor. You may find audience members who want to take over the discussion to the detriment of all participants—both those in the audience and those on the dais.

A moderator's success requires developing a relationship with and building the trust of the panelists. Developing trust takes time, but honesty, truthfulness, and living up to your promises are great places to start. Having the trust of your panelists permits you to ask them meaningful and engaging questions that will deliver the best panel experience for the audience. You must ensure the spotlight is on each panelist when they are speaking and that they feel as though they are being heard.

With this foundation, you can maintain an essential connection with your panelists. Otherwise, the entire experience risks being mediocre. It doesn't mean it will be a terrible panel, but rather an uphill battle to host a fabulous panel that gets a five-star rating from the audience.

Being a moderator is akin to being a tightrope walker. There are competing responsibilities that the moderator must balance.

> It is like being an orchestra conductor. You get to hone in on certain sections.
>
> —STEPHEN GROVE, VICE PRESIDENT, GLOBAL DIVERSITY AND INCLUSION, BLACKSTONE

A moderator must balance the desire to make the panelists look good with the fact that assuaging a panelist's ego is not the goal. It is a delicate dance, but one a great moderator learns how to do well. Learning how to make panelists look good while ensuring the audience is learning from the panelists and remains engaged in the discussion is a tightrope walk that great moderators have mastered. As a moderator, do not try to be the smartest person in the room. It will create defensive panelists and make everyone—the panelists and audience members—feel uncomfortable.

As a moderator, you enter unknown territory. A moderator needs to be adaptable and able to handle various situations that arise during the session. From technical difficulties and awkward panelists to unruly audience members, a great moderator can seamlessly and without fanfare work to ensure the panel continues progressing. You can imagine the perfect panel, but until you are on stage and asking panelists questions and hearing their responses, you will not know whether the panel will go well or poorly. For example, an extrovert over the phone may turn out to be an introvert when they are onstage in front of an audience. Or you may have someone who completely deviates from the topic. Learning how to handle these situations differentiates a good moderator from a bad one.

The panel moderator sets the tone for the overall panel. Emotions and how you deal with them profoundly impact your effectiveness as a moderator. Your emotions may be triggered by what a panelist says during the panel. Although emotions such as sadness, happiness, genuine concern, or even delight are easy to manage, feelings of anger, frustration, and distrust might occur, and you will need to learn how to conceal those during the panel discussion. You are like a therapist who doesn't react to what their patient tells them. A therapist absorbs the information and keeps the session moving right along. It is helpful to know in advance how you most effectively handle difficult situations when your emotions are more likely to come into play.

In a best-case scenario, you want to learn how to use these emotions productively. Feelings of joy, happiness, and delight are relatively easy to handle because you can channel these feelings into more energy and excitement for the panel. The more challenging emotions, those that occur when you strongly disagree with something a panelist or audience member says, are more challenging to control. However, it is important to control and channel these negative emotions and be conscious not to react. If you feel the audience is having the same emotional reaction to the panelists as you are or you feel there is the potential for an audience member to become disruptive, interrupt the panelist and steer the conversation to one of the many other questions you have prepared.

Although the intent of this book is to provide guidelines, there are no hard and fast rules. Using the approach to moderating outlined in this book will provide a structure to guide your behavior, the panelists' behavior, and the rules of engagement and to meet, if not exceed, audience expectations. It is a systematic approach to moderating panels to maximize the audience experience and takeaways. This book incorporates the advice of many expert moderators, whose thoughts, comments, tips, and strategies for being an effective panel moderator are shared throughout the text.

Being a moderator enables you to connect with the audience in a meaningful way. You need to understand that you have been given a lot of power over the panel and the audience's experience. And as Spiderman was told, "With great power comes great responsibility." You should take your power and use it to your best advantage.

Don't abuse your power by using the panel as a platform to express your personal views on a topic. They didn't ask you to be a keynote speaker! The organizers of the event have carefully curated the experience for their attendees. They have spent hours ensuring they have the right mix of panels and keynote speeches. Event organizers have reviewed the biographies and experiences of everyone they have invited to speak to ensure they have diverse perspectives and good balance. Adding your own views could be disruptive.

Moderating a panel can be a tough job. But there are great rewards from overseeing an engaging conversation with panelists who leave the panel satisfied with the experience and an audience that leaves having benefited from listening to and engaging in a dynamic conversation that has given them new insights and ideas they can share with others. A great moderator will be proud of their achievements.

> As a moderator you cultivate relationships and learn more about a subject matter that you may already know very well.
> —JOYCE CHANG, MANAGING DIRECTOR AND CHAIR, GLOBAL RESEARCH, JPMORGAN

> The best experiences that I have in moderating panels occur when you can inspire everyone in the room to really dig deep into the why of what they're doing.
> —NICOLE VALENTINE, FINTECH DIRECTOR, MILKEN INSTITUTE

Finally, the most critical piece of advice you should keep in mind as you read this book is this: a moderator is the audience's advocate.

1

WHY YOU NEED A PANEL HOW-TO GUIDE

This book is a reference guide—a tool a moderator can refer to along their moderator journey.

Why do you need a how-to guide for panel moderating? It seems like a skill one is born with or can pick up quickly. I think the difference between being a good moderator and being a great one is like the difference between someone who is a cook and someone who is a chef. I like to think of moderators as contestants who are competing in the television show *Top Chef*.

The chef and their ingredients are just like the moderator and the panelists. Contestants on *Top Chef* are given a basket of ingredients from which to prepare a meal for the judges. The ingredients are a surprise. Imagine opening the basket and, inside, you find a bottle of red wine, a filet mignon, and asparagus as your mystery ingredients. With that base, it's easy to make a fabulous meal regardless of whether you are a chef or a cook.

But on *Top Chef*, not all baskets are easy. What happens if you open the basket and find chicken, heart of palm, and coffee liqueur? The ingredients are all from the same categories as the first basket (one meat, one alcoholic drink, and one vegetable), but determining a way to blend all those ingredients and construct a great meal will be more demanding. A chef might look at the ingredients and instantaneously think of a recipe, but for a cook, having a cookbook by your side that you can use to look for similar recipes and adapt them would undoubtedly make the job easier.

This book is your cookbook for panel preparation.

STRUCTURE OF THIS GUIDE

Ideally, you will have read this book before being asked to be a moderator. This book covers what a moderator is, what characteristics make a good moderator, and most importantly, what questions to ask and what to consider before agreeing to be a moderator. Even if you have already agreed to be or have already been a moderator, this book is still a helpful guide because it will inform your process and make you a better moderator.

Reading this book from start to finish in one session is not required. You might be moderating a preassembled panel. In this case, you can probably skip some of the parts about recruiting potential panelists and assembling a diverse panel. However, even then, you might look at the panel, see it lacks diversity, and want to recommend a panel addition. You might initially skim some sections and return to them when they are more relevant. For example, you might wait to read the section about what to do on the day of the panel until the week before your panel, so the information is fresh in your mind as you begin your preparations.

This book has three parts:

1. Before the Panel

    These tasks should be completed well before the day of the panel. Some of them must happen before others. Before the event, you must invite your guests, familiarize yourself with them, and introduce the panelists to one another. Much of the prepanel work centers around recruiting, gathering information, coordinating schedules, and making your panelists feel comfortable—with you as the moderator, with the questions, with the format of the panel, and with the other panelists.

Getting the timing of all these parts right can be like managing a project. Individual panelist preparation calls must happen before you bring all the panelists together on one group call. But other parts of the prepanel work can be done at your own pace, including background reading and preparing questions for the panel.

2. During the Panel

The day of the event will be busy, and we have designed a series of checklists to help you plan and organize for it. These checklists will help you prepare so you are ready to handle anything that could go wrong on the day of the event.

The section discussing what could happen during the panel reviews many potential panel hiccups—from technology issues to unruly audience members and other situations that can and will go wrong on the day. If you have read in advance about how to handle these situations, you will be much better prepared to deal with them when you are on stage and all eyes are on you. Determining how to act under pressure before the situation arises is the best preparation.

3. After the Panel

Once you step off the stage, there are still actions a great moderator does that ensure the event continues to have an impact afterward. The postpanel section addresses these actions.

TEMPLATES AND CHECKLISTS

Multiple templates and examples throughout this book guide you through the moderating process and make your job as moderator and the preparation work more effortless. These templates include the following:

- Moderator Time Calculator
- Sample Panelist Ask Email
- Social Media and Event Promotion Guide
- Question Template
- Sample Opening Remarks
- Speaker Brief

In addition to these templates, you will find checklists throughout this book. These checklists should make moderating a panel easier, but they don't replace reading the accompanying sections. They are designed to ensure you don't forget to do something at critical moments, particularly during prep calls or just before you arrive on stage. The checklists contained in this book include the following:

- Questions to Ask Before Accepting
- Preacceptance
- Understanding the Audience
- Individual Prepanel Prep Call
- Group Prepanel Prep Call
- What to Bring to the Panel
- Panelist Prestage
- Moderator Prestage
- Postpanel

Moderating a panel is like "curating an experience for your audience," according to Sean Brown, director of Global Marketing and Communications at McKinsey & Company. These checklists and templates will make your role as moderator easier, ensuring that you don't miss necessary steps in the process.

SIDE BAR: THE POWER OF CHECKLISTS

Throughout this book, we have incorporated checklists you can use during your moderator planning to ensure that you cover everything you need before the panel, during panel precalls, before you go on stage, and after the event.

The power of the checklist is immense. Think about the airline pilot. They have undergone years of training before stepping into the cockpit as the primary pilot who is going to fly the plane. But despite all this training, they still have to complete a pretakeoff checklist every time they take the plane into the air. Why? By using a checklist, they aren't leaving anything to chance.

For you as a moderator, checklists will help reduce your stress because they give you a way of ensuring that you are asking all the questions you need to ask. Having prepanel call checklists ensures that you cover all the topics you need on a preprep call or an introductory call with a panelist and that you won't need to go back to the panelist with follow-up questions. On the day of the event, having a checklist means you have all the materials you need before you get up on stage.

A checklist does not take the intellectual rigor out of moderating a panel. Instead, it makes you less stressed because you are better prepared. Before the panel, it will allow you to focus more time on developing exciting questions that will draw out the best answers from the panelists that are informative and engaging for your audience. It will allow you to relax on stage and engage with your panelists rather than simply interviewing them.

WHO THIS BOOK IS FOR

Why do we need a book about how to moderate a panel effectively? There are thousands of blog posts, articles, and even videos you can download or read about how to moderate a panel. There are "Ten Tips for Moderating a Panel," "Tips for First Time Panelists," and "How to be a Great Moderator." Each provides good but often conflicting advice on what makes a great moderator. Sometimes, they even discuss some of the things terrible moderators do.

These books, articles, and posts are missing a key ingredient—comprehensiveness. They address part of the panel but not the entirety of it. They provide tips on assembling a panel but don't tell you how to prepare your panelists for the event. Many fail to discuss how to handle the inevitable hiccups all great moderators have had to handle at some point during their moderator careers.

Over the years, I have provided tips and advice to people who are looking to moderate panels, many of them rookies who had been asked to step into the role—either as part of their firm's marketing efforts or as part of an organization's effort to increase their firm's visibility. Being tapped as a moderator can expand a high-potential employee's role at an organization. However, not all moderators are asked to moderate a panel for the exposure it provides. Often it is simply because someone thought they would be effective and asked them.

For inexperienced moderators, this book is a comprehensive guide to panel moderation, guiding the reader through the process from start to end. It is a one-stop shop for anyone asked to moderate a panel. This book provides a step-by-step guide to organizing, preparing, and moderating a panel. We will teach you the tools and tricks to make your panel better, more engaging, and more energetic for the audience and the panelists and will provide you with moderating skills that are best in class.

For more experienced moderators, this book should elevate your skills and turn your good panels into great panels. Some of the tips seem obvious, but this book also identifies various best practices you might not be aware of. It also introduces the Speaker Brief (also known as a show-flow or run of show), which is a document often missing from most panel preparations. This brief can be distributed to your panelists before the event so everyone is on the same page, literally, before the event. Once you have read this book, I hope you will continue to refer to it and consider it a "best practice" guide to moderating a panel.

For organizations, we recommend you give this book to everyone you ask to moderate a panel on your behalf to help make your panels more effective. Many organizations use panels as a way of providing information to members, audiences, and potential clients. This book should be a go-to guide that organizers provide to every moderator before they agree to moderate a panel on the organization's behalf. Remember, while independent of your organization, the moderator is still a reflection of it. The returns from helping your moderators elevate their moderating skills could be immense and create significant value as the organization begins hosting expertly moderated events. The audience will learn more, appreciate the organization more, be more likely to return, and be grateful you did not waste their time.

For organizations that professionally organize events that include panels, this book can help you guide your panel moderators through the process. A well-trained group of moderators should increase attendance at your events as word spreads about the quality of your event. Developing a core competency by having well-prepared and trained moderators can also help your organization develop a deeper roster of panelists. These panelists will be happy to be invited back, having left with a positive panel experience. Additionally, because the expert community is a small and connected network, these satisfied panelists will likely refer you to other panelists and recommend your organization to them.

Reading this book can help many people. It isn't just for moderators. It is also for panelists, with a separate chapter addressing how panelists should prepare for their experience. I have been a panelist multiple times and have learned from these experiences about what works and what doesn't. A good panelist knows what to expect from the panel, is ready to answer questions relevant to their expertise, and can provide information that meets the audience's needs. These prepared panelists do a better job than their unprepared counterparts.

PREPARATION IS THE KEY

A moderator has positive energy, and they approach the panel like a conversation. They are very well prepared.
—Shari Krull, Chief Executive Officer, Streetwise Partners

The level of preparation can come through pretty clearly—either on the part of the moderator or on the part of the panelists, which is why we make it such a priority.
—Sean Brown, Director, Global Marketing
and Communications, McKinsey & Company

Preparation is vital for successful panels. Both prepared panelists and a prepared moderator make for an outstanding panel. Preparation makes the dialogue more fun and engaging. A moderator who has taken the time to get to know their panelists, their areas of expertise, and how to meld all these components into an engaging discussion is essential. It is the thoughtfulness and quality of the time you spend preparing, not the quantity of time.

Most people and organizations underestimate the importance of having a great moderator. Imagine how much better their events would be if they had provided training to the moderators to ensure the events reached their full potential. It is easy to assume a panel is just an open-format discussion between experts and that things will quickly fall into place without preparation. But this assumption is frequently incorrect because a panel engaging in a free-for-all conversation will often go off on tangents, undermining your ability to achieve the panel's mission.

Challenging panelists, unexpected answers, and unruly audiences are part of life and can derail a panel. As a moderator, you will need to think on your feet, and we will teach you how to prepare. We have included many tips from expert moderators, people who have been repeatedly asked to moderate panels for a multitude of event types and formats.

The checklists and templates provided throughout this book will systemize the process and ensure you don't get off a call and say, "I wish I had asked the panelist to send me this." These checklists should ensure you have everything you need for a successful event.

Sometimes, you might not ask a panelist for everything on the list. For example, if they have a biography on their firm's website, you might ask them if you can use it in the event's promotional materials rather than asking them to send their biography. That said, as a moderator, you should never assume anything, and if in doubt, ask. By asking whether you can use the biography, you are providing an opening to decide whether they want to go with their standard biography or provide you with a biography tailored to your panel audience.

There is no one right way to be a panel moderator. You should bring your best self and your original self to the panel. Be authentic to your style. Know your emotional triggers and topics that could derail you as the moderator. The advice, checklists, and pro forma guides are guides and can be customized to meet the needs of your panel.

There are two goals of any panel that a moderator must be laser focused on in terms of their achievement. First, the audience must have a positive experience and get what they came for, and second, the panelists should have a positive and fun experience.

So, it is time to start on the fun-filled journey to becoming a well-prepared moderator.

2

WHAT IS A MODERATOR?

The job of a moderator is to ensure a discussion or debate is fair. A moderator, according to a crossword puzzle answer, is "a presiding officer, especially a chairman [sic] of a debate."[1] Synonyms for moderator include mediator, referee, peacemaker, pacifier, stabilizer, and soother. A moderator clearly understands the panel's purpose, and their goal is to ensure the panel achieves this purpose. They provide a calming influence to ensure panelists feel at ease and make the audience feel comfortable, all while facilitating a dialogue between the moderator and each panelist, among the panelists themselves, and potentially between the moderator, the panelist, and the audience.

A true moderator ensures the audience hears everyone's views, not just one. Moderators can promote some level of debate if the panelists agree to it in advance and as long the debate makes all of the panelists shine rather than elevates one panelist at the expense of others. If there is a debate, the

---

1. Sporcle, "A Presiding Officer Especially a Chairman of a Debate: Crossword Clue," https://www.sporcle.com/reference/clue/a-presiding-officer-especially-a-chairman-of-a-debate.

moderator is responsible for ensuring the debate is courteous and professional. A moderator may find themselves in a situation with diverse opinions on a topic or divergent meanings of a word or event. Addressing issues like this can make a panel discussion more exciting and engaging.

Asking open-ended questions ensures the most relevant information is shared. Sometimes, moderators must probe for more details to ensure the panel provides a well-balanced perspective. They also must ensure that everyone participates and gets an equal chance to speak. Moderators might have to challenge participants to draw out views on the topic or bring clarity. They should highlight any factors that qualify the opinion of one of the panelists so the audience can place the panelist's opinion in context. Moderators must keep the panel focused, and sometimes, they might have to intervene in the discussion to get the panel back on topic.

The best moderators are those everyone perceives as being objective or impartial. Much like Switzerland, they don't take sides. No matter how hard it may be, you must avoid allowing personal bias to influence the outcome of the panel discussion. Being objective doesn't mean you don't prefer one person's views over another's. It means that you can't "show" the audience you prefer one panelist's view during the panel or postpanel discussions.

Technical considerations are sometimes overlooked. A moderator controls the timing and pacing of the panel. They ensure the panel goes slowly enough for participants to absorb all the information but must keep everyone engaged. They might have to move things forward when the conversation drifts or the discussion moves to talk about minor, potentially less relevant issues. The moderator must get the panel back on track.

As the panel's leader, the moderator knows they are the supporting actor, not the main character. They don't want to outshine their guests. Just as a circus has a ringmaster, every panel needs a moderator. A moderator wears various hats leading up to the event and during and after the event. While not quite as involved as a master of ceremonies, the role of moderator can be expansive. Depending on the organization that has asked you to moderate a panel, your role may include the following:

- Recruiting panelists
- Preparing questions
- Helping prepare the panelists for the event
- Hosting the panel
- Following up after the panel

A great moderator makes this all look easy. They are relaxed, have fun, and are in control. They are getting the panelists to share opinions, views, and perspectives. But because experts make moderating look so easy, those with less experience have been surprised by the complexity and difficulty of the task. You need to possess good interpersonal skills and strong listening skills. In addition, you need to be nonjudgmental and adaptable. You never know what will go wrong on the day of the panel.

> I love moderating panels. It feels like I am hosting a cocktail party where it is my job to make everyone interact with each other. I love, love, love the challenge.
> —ALIX STEEL, TELEVISION ANCHOR, BLOOMBERG LLP

> At the end of a party, all you want is for everyone to have a good time. At the end of the panel, you want the audience to take away a few key messages.
> —DEIRDRE BOLTON, HEAD OF EXECUTIVE DEVELOPMENT, PROSEK PARTNERS

WHAT A MODERATOR IS NOT

Sometimes, it is easier to understand what something is by understanding what it is not. A moderator is not an interviewer or a panelist, although there may be some overlap between the roles. Understanding each of these similar but different roles provides a better understanding of the role of a moderator.

An interviewer is "the person who asks the questions during an interview."[2]

An interview "is a face-to-face meeting, especially for the purpose of obtaining a statement or for assessing the qualities of a candidate."[3]

There are lessons to be learned from the process of interviewing that are applicable to panel preparation. For example, Indeed's recruiting platform has provided tips to ensure its clients' hiring managers have conducted well-prepared interviews of potential job candidates. They took the time to lay out a list of qualities that make for a great interviewer.

However, an interview is a two-way exchange of information. In contrast, a panel discussion is broader, involving not only an exchange between the moderator and the panelist but also an exchange between the panelists themselves. A moderator is not an interviewer. They don't think of the panelists as interviewees and don't treat them as such. A moderator isn't looking to assess the qualities of a panelist. Instead, they are trying to elicit information from the panelist that will help the audience, having

---

2. Cambridge Dictionary, "Interviewer," https://dictionary.cambridge.org/dictionary/english/interviewer.
3. Oxford English Dictionary, "Interview," https://www.oed.com/dictionary/interview_n?tab=meaning_and_use.

already ascertained the credentials and expertise of the panelist beforehand.

Good interviewers prepare for their interviews. If you have ever interviewed for a job, it is very easy to determine whether the interviewer came prepared—it is easy to ascertain if they read your cover letter and resumé before starting the interview and whether they are asking questions off the cuff or have a list they composed in advance of the interview.

Learning to write and ask great questions is a talent that is important for great interviewers and great moderators alike. Asking thoughtful questions makes an interview and panel better. Good interviews should follow a structure—the same way you will need to determine the structure of your panel. It is an important skill to master if you want to moderate a panel successfully.

Listening is a skill we all need to master. An interviewer should be a good listener. They want to find out whether the candidate has the skills to do the job and is a cultural fit. Likewise, listening is critical for moderators. You will need to be listening all the time during prep calls, as you engage with the panel and audience, and as you collect postpanel feedback.

An interviewer must never forget they are not the central character in the interview—the interviewee is. Similarly, the moderator is not the central character of a moderated panel.

In today's war for talent, interviews are no longer one-way streets. An interviewer's role is to "softly" sell the company and the role to the candidate. This is where interviews and panels differ. Moderating a panel does not involve this type of sales pitch.

Finally, the ability to solicit feedback is another difference between the role of an interviewer and a moderator. There is less of a feedback loop during the interview process, whereas feedback from panelists, support staff, and the audience is a key dimension at the end of a panel to continue to improve. An interviewer cannot ask an interviewee for honest postinterview feedback because that feedback will be tainted depending on whether the interviewee was offered the job.

A facilitator is also not a moderator. Facilitators lead focus groups. The term "focus group" in the United States describes group discussions and in-depth research into consumer habits and attitudes. The term is interpreted and used much more broadly outside the United States, which includes the discussion of organizational issues and problem-solving and can also be used to determine the attitudes and morale of a group. Based on the dictionary definition of facilitate, a facilitator is a person who makes a process easier.

Despite the tendency to confuse the two roles, the roles played by a facilitator and a moderator differ. But just like interviewing tips can help moderators improve their moderating skills, understanding the role of a facilitator and the characteristics that define a good facilitator can help improve your skills as an effective moderator.

Facilitators make the process of a focus group session go more smoothly and guide a team through a predetermined process. A facilitator asks open-ended questions and assists the group in remaining focused to fulfill its objectives. The facilitator will do their best to ensure the group collaborates and collectively does their best work together. A facilitator also performs the role of making sure the group stays on topic and ensures the group does not get waylaid by group politics or begin to suffer from groupthink. If a conflict arises, the facilitator may need to deescalate it so the group can move forward. A facilitator helps the team perform at their best, gently nudging the group in the right direction, and when they get off course, the facilitator, by asking pertinent questions, can help the group get back on track.

Participants in a facilitated session and panelists on a panel have skills and qualifications relevant to the session or topic. However, in contrast to a panelist, a facilitated session participant does not need to have a particular angle on a topic.

A facilitator sees their role as helping the group arrive at a collective solution to a problem by assisting the group and providing tools and techniques to help them engage efficiently toward their end goal. This process is to help the team members leverage their skills in creative ways to achieve an optimal solution.

In addition, a facilitator doesn't need to be enthusiastic about the topic. Still, they have the energy and personality to drive the group forward and ensure the room's energy doesn't experience the typical lull. In contrast, a great moderator is enthusiastic about the topic, and this enthusiasm is contagious. Your interest in the topic, be it a professional interest or a personal interest, was probably the reason you were asked to moderate the panel in the first place.

Similarly, if the group's energy is waning, a facilitator will do something to energize the group. It could be as simple as asking participants to stand up and shaking their bodies for a few moments or, in the event of a more extended session, taking a ten-minute break to use the facilities, taking a short trip outside to get some fresh air, or taking a break from "think work." As a moderator, you can't suggest the panelists take a ten-minute energy break during the panel, so you must think of other ways to energize a fading panel.

The traits that make an excellent facilitator are similar to those of a good moderator. Both must determine whether something is inconsequential (I can hear a sigh of relief) or needs to be addressed. Time management, adaptation, and managing unruly or unproductive participants are all similar skills shown by good moderators and good facilitators. Both must ensure all team members or panelists participate and adapt if things go awry. Facilitators must deal with rowdy participants, just as a moderator must address rowdy audience members, and get the group or the panel back on track.

Finally, a moderator isn't a panelist. Hopefully that should be obvious, but it is worth stressing. A moderator must manage the panel process and the dynamics of the panel. They must use their position to influence the panelists to ensure the panel meets its purpose. That responsibility requires a high degree of neutrality by the moderator to ensure that their views do not monopolize the conversation and the views of the panelists are heard.

As a moderator, do not involve yourself in the debate, even when you are in disagreement or agreement with the panelists. This will completely throw the panel off track. Overemphasizing one panelist's point of view is humiliating for the other panelists, suggesting they are secondary players at the event. It's a lose–lose for everyone. Understanding the difference between the two roles of moderator and panelist is essential because no one wants their moderator to be a quasi-panelist and vice versa nobody wants panelists who act as though they are moderating the panel.

CHARACTERISTICS OF A GREAT MODERATOR

A truly great moderator gets the talkers to listen and the listeners to talk.

—Ranji Nagaswami, finance industry leader, chief executive and chief investment officer of leading global asset management firms, and chief investment advisor to Mayor Michael Bloomberg

Being a great moderator gives you the opportunity to let other people come alive.
—Ellen Carr, Portfolio Manager, Barksdale & Co., and adjunct professor at Columbia Business School

The following is a list of characteristics I have consistently identified among great moderators. Although some of these characteristics might appear obvious, I have been surprised how often moderators lack them. The characteristics of great moderators include the following:

- *Unobtrusive*: The objective of a moderator is to guide the conversation, not dominate it. This means assisting the panelists when needed and moving the panel discussion forward in an unnoticeable way.
- *Humility*: A great moderator knows they are not the person to whom the audience came to listen. They are humble and are able to showcase others.
- *Energetic*: The energy exuded by an energetic moderator is contagious, and both the panelists and the audience can sense it. Energetic does not mean loud. You don't have to scream like a coach on the sidelines of your kid's soccer game to be a great moderator. But dull, boring moderators do not capture the audience's attention and have trouble inciting excitement in their panelists.
- *Inquisitive*: A moderator wants to learn as much about the topic as the audience members. Curiosity, just like energy, is contagious.
- *Good listener*: This applies throughout the process of moderating a panel. As a moderator, you must listen constantly. As discussed, this starts during the preparation call as you listen to the topics your panelists want to discuss and address any

concerns before the day of the panel. During the panel, a moderator asks questions, listens to the answers, and leverages those answers throughout the discussion.

- *Good at summarizing*: Listening to a long answer to a question and then summarizing the key messages for the audience is a vital moderator skill.
- *A diligent timekeeper*: Keeping the panel on track and managing "airtime" for each panelist is a crucial role.
- *Fairness advocate*: A moderator knows when to redirect the panel. They also know when one panelist is taking over the panel and can redirect the conversation away from that person toward the other panelists to ensure everyone has a fair turn. They also bring into the conversation those who have said less than others on the panel.
- *Nonjudgmental*: A moderator can't censor or judge the panelists' responses. As mentioned earlier, a moderator is like Switzerland—objective and neutral.
- *Empathy*: When panelists share stories, particularly stories of hardship, a good moderator is an empathic listener. A great moderator has high emotional intelligence and lots of empathy.
- *Positive regard*: A moderator should hold each panelist in high regard regardless of whether they agree with the panelist's views. This positive regard should be evident from the introduction, questions, and question order.
- *Inclusive*: A moderator should acknowledge each panelist's contribution and seek to include all panelists in the discussion.
- *Neutral demeanor*: A moderator should be open to all opinions and not take a stance on a topic during the discussion. The moderator needs to balance their own verbal responses and nonverbal cues.
- *Flexible*: You never know what might go wrong—a panelist could cancel at the last minute or the technology might not work.

We'll give you tips to help handle these situations, but being adaptable in the face of adversity is a key trait that makes you a better moderator.

- *Good actor*: Being a good actor can help, but remember, you aren't the lead actor; you're an actor in a supporting role. Being happy to play "second fiddle" is a distinguishing feature of moderators.
- *Personable*: A moderator must establish rapport with the panelists and the audience. Being able to have good chemistry with the panelists helps. You should have a personality and be willing to let that shine through.
- *Feedback*: Some of the best moderators became great because they sought feedback on their performance and incorporated it into their next moderator engagement.

Which characteristics should you work on improving to improve your ability to moderate a panel? Some people advise you to focus on improving areas where you are weak, but I think you should focus on those characteristics where you shine and make those even better. Then bring those areas where you don't excel up to at least "average." There is much more to gain from getting better at the things you are already good at and spending less time fixing your weaker areas.

A great moderator knows when to step back. In recalling one of her most successful panels, Lisa Kaplowitz, an associate professor at Rutgers Business School and executive director of the Rutgers Center for Women in Business (CWIB), stated: "The panel was so amazing because neither of us was asking questions. The panelists were just talking and engaging, and the audience was contributing." Professor Kaplowitz was an invisible moderator, but it was her extensive preparation, knowledge of the topic, and her willingness to step in when needed that made this a very successful event.

As a moderator, you have the ability to make others shine. Tell your panelists this up front and repeat it often. The panel is about making the panelists look good, not the moderator. It is about the panelists and their experiences and sharing those experiences with the audience, giving them a new perspective, or helping to advance discussion on a topic.

THE IMPORTANCE OF A GOOD MODERATOR

Making a panel great when you have a mediocre moderator is an uphill battle. But making a mediocre group of panelists perform well is possible if a great moderator leads the discussion. As in life, learning helps. By picking up this book and reading it, even if you are only reading or revisiting a particular section, you are learning to be a better moderator. Keep learning because knowledge, too, will make you better.

Researchers agree on the importance of a great moderator:

> The skills and personality of the moderator cannot be overemphasized. . . . Their skills will influence the success of the discussion and the quality of the outcome.
>
> —FAITH GIBSON, SENIOR LECTURER[4]

---

4. Faith Gibson, "Conducting Focus Groups with Children and Young People: Strategies for Success," *Journal of Research in Nursing* 12, no. 5 (2007): 473–83, https://www.projectrise.eu/sites/default/files/documentation/2018-12/Journal%20of%20Research%20in%20Nursing-2007-Gibson-473-83_1.pdf.

The role of the moderator is very significant. Good levels of group leadership and interpersonal skills are required to moderate a group successfully.
—DR. ANITA GIBBS[5]

Speakers may draw the audience, but how the moderator orchestrates the session can make the difference between an event that is mediocre and one that is exciting, engaging, and productive for both audience and panelists. Making sure the panel discussion is enjoyable and effective requires advanced preparation.
—TEMERTY FACULTY OF MEDICINE AT THE UNIVERSITY OF TORONTO[6]

---

5. Anita Gibbs, "Focus Groups," *Social Research Update* 19 (1997), https://openlab.citytech.cuny.edu/her-macdonaldsbs2000fall2015b/files/2011/06/Focus-Groups_Anita-Gibbs.pdf.
6. Temerty Faculty of Medicine, "How to Be a Great Moderator," University of Toronto, 2020, 03-How-to-be-a-Great-Moderator.pdf (utoronto.ca).

3

BEFORE YOU ACCEPT THE ASSIGNMENT

Someone asks you to moderate a panel. This will benefit both you and the organization and help advance your career. But before you say yes, you should think about some essential factors. I don't want to discourage you from accepting the assignment, but I want you to have a realistic and detailed roadmap of what moderating a panel entails so you can decide based on all available information. Accepting the role and doing a terrible job can negatively affect everyone involved.

HAVING THE TIME TO DO THE JOB WELL

You have to prepare over a period of time. You can't rush it because that means you're just checking the box.
—Experienced Moderator

The most important question to ask yourself is whether you have time to moderate the panel and do it to a standard to which you would be proud. Thoughtfully moderating a panel is a significant commitment. Being a moderator involves more than just the hour you are on the stage. It includes the travel time, the buffer time, the preparation calls, the research time, and the time it will take you to develop questions and assemble an engaging panel. It is a multiple of the actual panel time for preparing questions, researching, and familiarizing yourself with the topic and panelists. There is also a lot of logistical work involved. As you think about preparing for a panel, you should understand the time commitment and make sure your schedule can accommodate it.

Moderating a panel is hard work, and remember, it may also be unpaid work. You might get kudos and exposure for moderating a panel, but it is often at the expense of your leisure time or other projects or assignments at work. You should also remember that the commitment doesn't happen all at once, so if you have agreed to multiple panels, you want to ensure they don't all "hit" simultaneously.

The Moderator Time Calculator template below and the example that I prepared for myself for a four-member hour long panel is provided to assist you in determining how much time it will take to moderate a panel and do it well. Remember the adage, "It always takes longer than you think."

MODERATOR TIME CALCULATOR

Research and identify potential panelists	❑ hours
Send emails to panelists	❑ hours
Confirm panelists and set up individual calls	❑ hours
Research panel topic	❑ hours
Promote panel on social media, etc.	❑ hours
Make individual panelist calls	❑ hours
Have group call	❑ hours
Prepare the Speaker Brief	❑ hours
Develop questions	❑ hours
Travel to panel and arrive early	❑ hours
Conduct panel	❑ hours
Send postpanel thank you notes	❑ hours
Engage in postpanel media	❑ hours
Total Estimated Time	❑ **hours**

The above Moderator Time Calculator should be helpful in calculating a panel's time commitment. Below is an example that I prepared for myself for a four-member panel.

Research and identify potential panelists	2 hours
Send emails to panelists	2 hours
Confirm panelists and set up individual calls	1 hour
Research panel topic	2 hours
Promote panel on social media, etc.	1 hour
Make individual panelist calls	4 hours
Have group call	1 hour
Prepare the Speaker Brief	3 hours
Develop questions	2 hours
Travel to panel and arrive early	1 hour
Conduct panel	1 hour
Send postpanel thank you notes	1 hour
Engage in postpanel media	2 hours
Total Estimated Time	**23 hours**

Can you streamline these tasks? Absolutely. The question is whether doing so would hurt your ability to be a great moderator, and based on my many years of experience, cutting short the preparation or cutting corners will undermine the panel's effectiveness. This book is about understanding the work that goes into being a great moderator and the time commitment involved and helping you make an informed decision. If you don't think you will be able to fully commit the time it requires to do the job well, then say no to the opportunity, if possible.

CONFLICTS OF INTEREST AND PURPOSE MISALIGNMENT

Not every opportunity will be the right opportunity for you as a moderator. For example, you must be comfortable that your values align with the panel's purpose. Or if you have a conflict of interest, you should immediately let the organizers know why you cannot accept. For example, if the panel's purpose is to promote a product in a market that your firm is considering entering, then saying no is the right thing to do. You don't need to disclose confidential information.

Use your judgment and don't feel bad about saying the opportunity is not a good fit because of these reasons. It is better to do so earlier rather than later.

QUESTIONS TO ASK BEFORE SAYING YES

There are many considerations before accepting to be a moderator beyond knowing and understanding the time commitment. Having answers to all of these questions is a key aspect of being an effective moderator. After confirming the time, date, and location of the panel and ensuring your availability, determine whether the event will be held in person or as a virtual panel. Importantly, ask whether the date might be subject to change in the future. After doing all the preparatory work, it is frustrating to later discover that the panel date has moved and you are no longer available. This is a frequent occurrence at multiday events.

There are several additional questions that you need to ask. Some of these questions are intuitive, but knowing the information in advance can make the difference between having a great experience and having a poor experience as a moderator. These questions are all included in the Questions to Ask Before Accepting checklist in this chapter. These questions should provide you with all the information you need to make an informed decision. Don't think that asking these questions is being intrusive or showing disinterest in moderating the panel. These questions show an organizer that you are taking this opportunity seriously. Once you have all the information, you can decide. You might want to phrase your initial response as follows: "I'm interested in moderating the panel you describe, but I have a couple of questions about it."

Do not be afraid to ask the conference organizers about travel and hotel reimbursement if you must travel a significant distance to the event, including the policy regarding expenses such as airfare, Uber rides, and cab fares. Ask if the firm intends to collect guests from their hotels, the airport, or their apartments or if you and the panelists should make your own arrangements to get to the panel location. There is no standard for travel reimbursement. Be aware that many organizations do not reimburse for travel (it has more to do with the fact they don't know where you will be traveling from and whether you are traveling via private jet or commercial airline than their being cheap with their expense reimbursement policy). Even if they don't cover airline travel, they might offer to provide you with accommodation free of charge at the conference hotel. It is to your advantage to know this information in advance.

Decide if you need to get permission to participate. Your firm may have media and communications policies that may preclude certain opportunities. Suppose the conference organizers want to record the panel. Are you okay with this? Is there a possibility there will be media in the audience? For both questions, check with your corporate communications department or someone with responsibility for those policies at your firm regarding whether you are allowed to moderate the panel. For corporate communication concerns, it is always better to ask for permission than to beg for forgiveness afterward.

You should update your estimate of the time involved in the panel based on some of the answers that you receive. For example, if the panel is in a different location than you expected (i.e., it involves a flight across the country), you should consider that. If necessary, ask the organizer to give you some time to consider it. If you ask the organizer for more time to decide, give them a specific date by which you will provide an answer and hold yourself to the commitment you have made.

Although it is an honor to be asked to moderate a panel, you need to know what you're getting into. What do they expect from you? Don't be afraid to ask questions. Asking questions doesn't mean you aren't interested. Instead, it signals that you want to learn more.

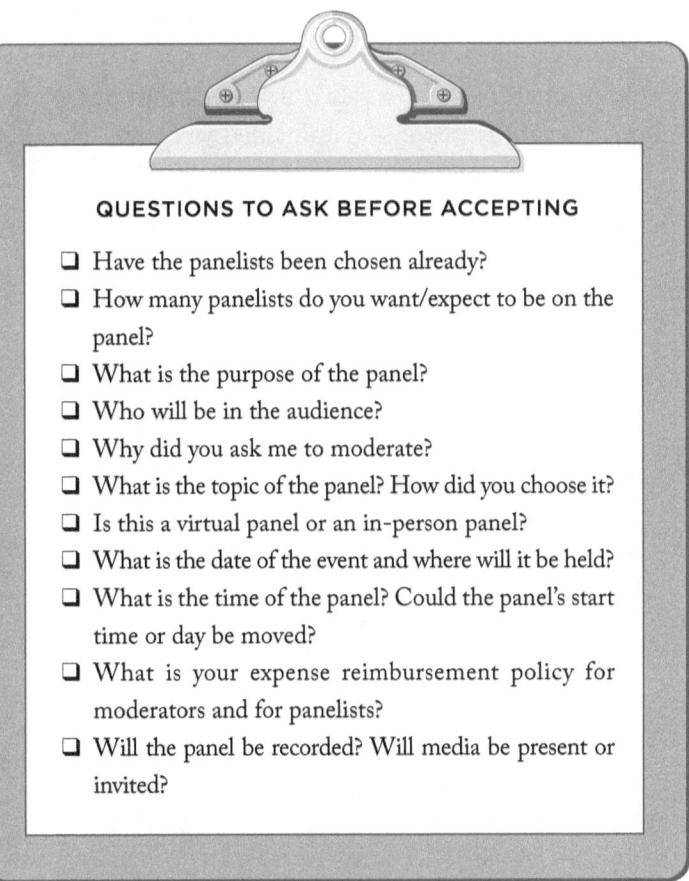

QUESTIONS TO ASK BEFORE ACCEPTING

- ❏ Have the panelists been chosen already?
- ❏ How many panelists do you want/expect to be on the panel?
- ❏ What is the purpose of the panel?
- ❏ Who will be in the audience?
- ❏ Why did you ask me to moderate?
- ❏ What is the topic of the panel? How did you choose it?
- ❏ Is this a virtual panel or an in-person panel?
- ❏ What is the date of the event and where will it be held?
- ❏ What is the time of the panel? Could the panel's start time or day be moved?
- ❏ What is your expense reimbursement policy for moderators and for panelists?
- ❏ Will the panel be recorded? Will media be present or invited?

THE CAREER BENEFITS OF BEING A MODERATOR

Someone asks you to moderate a panel, and based on everything you've just read, it seems like a lot of work. Having calculated the amount of time it will take to moderate the panel, you are questioning the benefits of saying yes.

We have found that there are many career benefits to moderating a panel. It immediately increases your visibility within the industry and, potentially, your company. Through the materials advertising the panel and your exposure during the event, increased visibility will help cement your expertise in the field and as a moderator.

It is a great networking opportunity because you meet new people as a moderator and gain a new perspective on a topic. Another benefit is that it highlights that you have knowledge on that topic.

> It increases visibility. It is good for your brand, internally and externally. It is important to your firm. You're carrying your own personal flag but also your brand's flag and your firm's flag.
> —DEIRDRE BOLTON, HEAD OF EXECUTIVE DEVELOPMENT, PROSEK PARTNERS

Others have noted the following benefits:

> The best part for me is getting to know each panelist on another level. It expands and deepens your relationship.
> —SARAH AUERBACH, MANAGING DIRECTOR, UNIFI BY CAIA

> The learning experience is actually the most enjoyable part for me.
> —JOANNA HOROWITZ, CFA, SENIOR CONSULTANT—ALTERNATIVE INVESTMENT ADVISORY AND CORPORATE RESPONSIBILITY AND DIVERSITY LEAD, BIP. MONTICELLO

Moderating is a great way to show superiors you can be both a team player and a coach. It showcases your ability to act in the best interests of others as a team member who can work with people from all walks of life, with different personalities, different backgrounds, divergent speaking styles, and interests. As you move up the organizational ladder, you need to move away from being seen as just an individual contributor, and seek opportunities to be viewed as a team leader. Being a moderator helps you on this journey.

Moderating a panel provides experience that is akin to managing a team. In fact, it is harder to manage a panel because the panelists are volunteers, which means they are not motivated by a paycheck. Your position as moderator will provide you with an opportunity to showcase your leadership skills and potential as you learn what motivates each panelist and how to leverage each of their strengths and offset each of their weaknesses to create the best team of panelists.

Developing relationships with panelists helps to expand your sphere of influence. You will develop new contacts both within and outside your industry. While this shouldn't be the key motivation for agreeing to moderate a panel, doing a great job moderating a panel may lead to other career opportunities for you.

As you develop your moderating expertise and experience, your executive presence will increase. Executive presence is that magnetic pull you have that draws people to you and that enhances individual trust in your leadership. Demonstrating the ability to command a panel of executives, thought leaders, or industry experts, particularly if they hold senior positions, will highlight your ability to develop executive presence. Being a prepared and effective moderator will allow your self-assurance to shine through.

Consider inviting your manager or someone higher up in your organization to attend the panel so they can see you in action, particularly your skills as a public speaker. Your role in your organization might not have yet afforded such an opportunity. Many people shy away from public speaking, but as the panel's moderator, you can highlight your abilities from the opening speech to introductions, panelist questions, and facilitating audience questions. These skills will set you apart from others in your organization who haven't had similar opportunities.

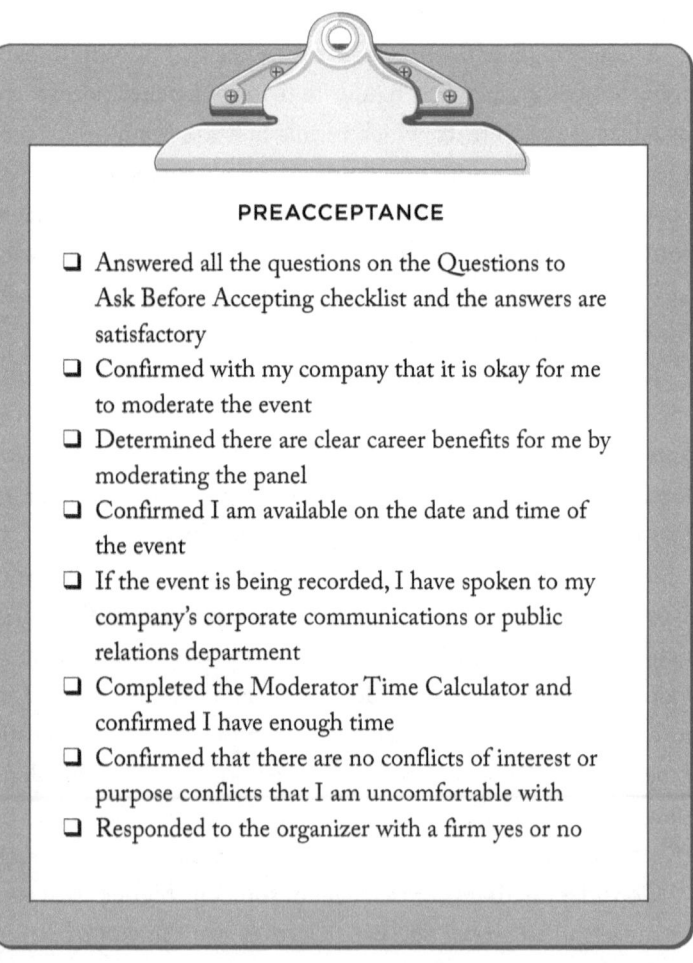

PREACCEPTANCE

- ❏ Answered all the questions on the Questions to Ask Before Accepting checklist and the answers are satisfactory
- ❏ Confirmed with my company that it is okay for me to moderate the event
- ❏ Determined there are clear career benefits for me by moderating the panel
- ❏ Confirmed I am available on the date and time of the event
- ❏ If the event is being recorded, I have spoken to my company's corporate communications or public relations department
- ❏ Completed the Moderator Time Calculator and confirmed I have enough time
- ❏ Confirmed that there are no conflicts of interest or purpose conflicts that I am uncomfortable with
- ❏ Responded to the organizer with a firm yes or no

DECLINING AN OPPORTUNITY

Sometimes, you will have to decline the opportunity. After saying no to an organizer, consider recommending an alternative moderator to them (and even suggest they read a copy of this book!). This is entirely within your discretion, but it can generate goodwill with conference organizers and could result in your being asked to moderate a different panel.

4

PREPANEL PLANNING

Now that you know how a moderator functions and have accepted the role of panel moderator, the rest of this book will take you from start to finish in terms of planning your panel from the prepanel conversations to the day of the event and through postevent activities.

Addressing each stage of preparation is crucial. If you don't adequately prepare for a panel, you set yourself and the panel up for failure. But even excellent preparation cannot overcome poor execution on the day of the event, and even when the panel is over, you can take actions to ensure you get asked to moderate another panel. If everyone leaves the event feeling as though it was a success, you will know that you prepared correctly.

CHOOSING A PANEL TOPIC

The panel topic must be relevant and topical. It does not need to be controversial to generate audience interest, but it should be a topic the audience will want to talk to other people about. You want a topic that will serve the audience rather than the sponsors of the panel or the panelists themselves.

Although this might seem challenging, you want the audience to learn something from the panel—something they will want to remember.

Although not always the case, often a moderator can influence the topic of the panel or can help narrow a broad topic. As you think about this task, I suggest developing a topic that is interesting to your audience and, more importantly, that is also highly engaging. The sign of a successful panel is when audience members can't wait to share the information they learned or the panel's conclusions with someone else.

When brainstorming a panel topic, consider asking a question or defining a problem, and then work to ensure your panel either answers the question asked or provides a solution to the identified problem. The panel should not be about a thing (i.e., zebras) but rather about an issue or idea related to it (i.e., Why are zebras at risk of extinction in Africa?). Although your panel might be meant to educate people about a topic, it will be far more impactful if you both educate them about the problem and provide them with opportunities and ways they can help. This makes the panel more memorable.

UNDERSTANDING THE PURPOSE OF THE PANEL

What is it that I want people to walk away from this conversation with?

—Stephen Grove, Vice President, Global Diversity and Inclusion, Blackstone

As mentioned earlier, a panel discussion should be tied to a mission or purpose. Without a purpose, little will be achieved and the panel will sound like nothing more than a friendly chat. Be very clear about the panel's purpose and ensure panelists are aligned with that purpose. This will help in selecting panelists, devising questions, and framing the discussion more generally. Clarifying the purpose will ensure you meet the needs of the most discerning customers in the room: the audience.

Sharing the panel's purpose with the panelists before they agree to be a panel member will transform the panel's mission and purpose into a shared vision of the event that everyone can rally around. It will help panelists as they prepare for the event and will help you develop questions for the panelists. You should also consider sharing the purpose of the panel with the audience ahead of time to set audience expectations.

Panel discussion objectives often include the following:

- *Sales*: Many panels are designed to promote a product, a book, a service, or even an app. Here the purpose of the panel is to influence the audience's decision-making process. Panels that have a sales objective are often best received when the product that is being promoted is new and innovative because the audience often perceives the panel discussion as being educational rather than promotional.
- *Information*: An informational panel can be helpful when addressing a topic that is difficult to understand because, unlike podcasts, the panel provides audience members with opportunities to ask clarificatory questions. For example, blockchain was a confusing technology when first introduced. Many organizations—from investment banks to venture capital firms—hosted panels to inform audiences of the technology's features, benefits, and drawbacks.
- *Raising awareness*: Nonprofit organizations often host panels to raise awareness of a particular issue important to their

cause, such as parenting in the digital age. Any parent with children as young as age two to teenagers is likely interested in learning more about the topic. However, parenting in a digital age isn't just an issue for parents. It is an issue for nonprofits that provide services to children and teens with other issues (e.g., temporarily separated from their families). Everyone who interacts regularly with a child can learn more on this topic. Hosting a panel of technology experts, social workers, and parents can provide perspectives on the issue and help the audience feel more connected with the children and teens served by the nonprofit because they see them facing the same issues their children face.

- *Membership building*: A membership organization might host a panel to raise awareness of the organization among non-members. Such a panel would be considered a "teaser" because it tries to drive some audience members to join the organization to access similar content through digital platforms, other panel opportunities, and publications.
- *Continuing education*: Many professional organizations have a minimum continuing professional education (CPE) requirement, and panels are often an excellent way for members to meet those membership requirements. Depending on the organization, you might need to submit an outline of the panel to qualify for the CPE credit based on the rules of the organization granting the credits. The outlines usually include information regarding the topics to be covered, the "learning outcome," and the length of the panel. Advertising that your audience members will receive CPE credit is also good to include when marketing the panel.
- *Fundraising and friend raising*: Some organizations will host a panel for their fundraising efforts. They will look to find a topic to highlight their vital work. A panel could highlight

how to rebuild an economy, city, or country after a natural disaster. At the end of the panel, after the audience question-and-answer session, a representative from the organization might come forward and offer the audience various ways they can help—through volunteering, providing professional expertise, or donating money or particular items (e.g., blankets, canned goods).

Some panels have multiple purposes and objectives. In this situation, as a moderator, you should identify the primary purpose of the panel and then, if necessary, identify the secondary purpose. A panel should not have more than a primary and secondary purpose—if you find yourself in this dilemma, seek to prioritize just two purposes. An example of a multipurpose panel could be a nonprofit that wants to tell parents how important it is to understand technology's positive impact on a child's education. That would be the primary purpose of the panel—raising awareness of the issue. A secondary purpose, as long as the organizer is aligned with this objective, could be fundraising.

CHOOSING A TITLE FOR YOUR PANEL

Having an exciting and memorable title for your panel is imperative. You need to use active words and spark curiosity. Don't make the title of the panel vague. Make it interesting. Instead of discussing "digital devices and children," ask a provocative question and then have panelists discuss all sides of the issue. "Should your three-year-old child be allowed to play on your phone?" is a much better topic of discussion, and there will be some who answer "yes," some who answer a definitive "no," and potentially some who say "sometimes." Those three answers will make for an engaging conversation.

A thought-provoking panel title will make promoting and marketing your panel effortless. It is better to take the time up front to think of a good title rather than quickly choosing a title and regretting it later. Searching the Internet or using generative AI can provide you with inspiration for a title.

Before you finalize your panel title, you should also use the Internet to check whether another similar organization has used the title in the past. Although imitation may be considered flattery, you don't want people to confuse your organization and your panel with another organization and their panel.

UNDERSTANDING THE AUDIENCE

When I'm moderating, I am always, always, always thinking about the audience. I feel very strongly about that. All of us, the moderator and the panelists, are there in service of the audience.

—Deirdre Bolton, Head of Executive Development, Prosek Partners

To be an effective moderator, you must understand who the intended audience is. You want a panel focused on the audience, ensuring they have a great experience and that the information they learn at the discussion is relevant and informative. Finally, you want to deliver the content in the most user-friendly way.

Marketers do a great job of understanding their customers and their audience, and there is a lot we can learn from them. In marketing, the customer or user experience is one of the most critical metrics, and in panel discussions, the audience experience is an important and often underappreciated consideration. To have a successful panel, you must understand your panel customers, i.e., the audience. Without an audience, there would be no panel.

Who is in the audience? What do you want their experience to be? What are their expectations?

Learning about your audience's interests can also be informative as you consider the panel questions. It helps if you have spoken with the conference or panel sponsor or organizer about who they expect to be in the audience and who they are targeting with the panel. This question is linked, in many respects, to the panel's purpose.

As part of your due diligence, you asked about the audience before accepting the opportunity to moderate. So after you begin researching the topic and forming your panel, you should find time to ask the conference organizers more questions about the audience. Some of this information should be readily available, and some may not be if, for example, the conference organizers are waiting for more people to accept the invitation to join the conference before they provide you with relevant data.

Find out whether there are statistics or characteristics that describe the audience. Request a copy of the data he event planner has collected regarding audience members' job functions, their years in their current job or in the industry, and if relevant, the industry in which they work. You might be able to obtain location information, which is often helpful—for example, knowing whether the audience is local or international impacts your speaking pace.

The best panels cater to their audience. The more you know about the audience, the more you can tailor the panelists and discussion to their needs. Analyze your audience and try to understand them. Only some of the data you want about your panel will be available, but this is a situation where the more data, the better. If you are moderating an educational panel, is this an audience where a free trial or download of your product would be useful or helpful? Should you have information cards available for them to take away? You should analyze and think about your audience in the most basic ways. Even though this is a panel, it is similar to a presentation because you need to understand your audience and their needs. You might not be able to get statistics about your audience, but any data you can obtain about the target of panel outreach and who signed up should be helpful as you prepare your questions. For example, I have often moderated panels in the finance industry, and knowing how many allocators versus financial advisors and company employees are in the audience helps me prioritize the questions so they are relevant to the greatest number of audience members.

Technology can also make your panel more engaging for the audience. For example, I have seen a moderator ask a question of the audience at the beginning of a panel and project the answers in the form of a word cloud onto a screen in real time. You could consider a similar experience. If you are talking about a new way of doing surgery and you are speaking to prospective surgeon customers, you might ask them what words come to mind when they think about the current surgery technology. You can have everyone use phones during a panel for phone polling on a question. Many applications are available that can enable you to do this simply and inexpensively (often for free). Polling the audience can help you understand if the audience has any preconceived biases that you might need to debunk for your panel to be successful.

You should acknowledge differences in the audience and celebrate these differences. Is your conference centered around bringing together two groups with different ideas who want to cooperate? They could be supporters of a think tank with left- or right-leaning tendencies who have come together to explore solutions to poverty, opportunity, or homelessness. As a moderator, you should be up front and transparent and address these differences among the panelists, the audience members, or both. You should then say something to ensure the audience realizes you are a neutral party for the panel. You could say something like, "We have both self-identifying Democrats and Republicans on this panel. Although the panelists may voice views that identify with their political affiliation, we are here today to use this panel to jump-start our brainstorming sessions, which will happen immediately following the conclusion of the panel. We would prefer if you don't let someone's political leaning detract from you hearing about different ways our community could address the current homeless population."

After learning as much as possible about the audience, a great moderator will set goals for how they intend to meet the audience's needs. It is important to articulate these goals up front. After the panel, survey the audience to see if your panel met those goals as you defined them. Thinking in this way is what distinguishes a great moderator. When you think about your audience, what do you want the panelists to say to them? What do you want the key takeaways to be? What is the main idea behind the panel? Do the panelists need data to back up their points? Answering these questions before you build your panel, develop questions, and finalize your topic will ensure your audience leaves the event feeling like it was time very well spent.

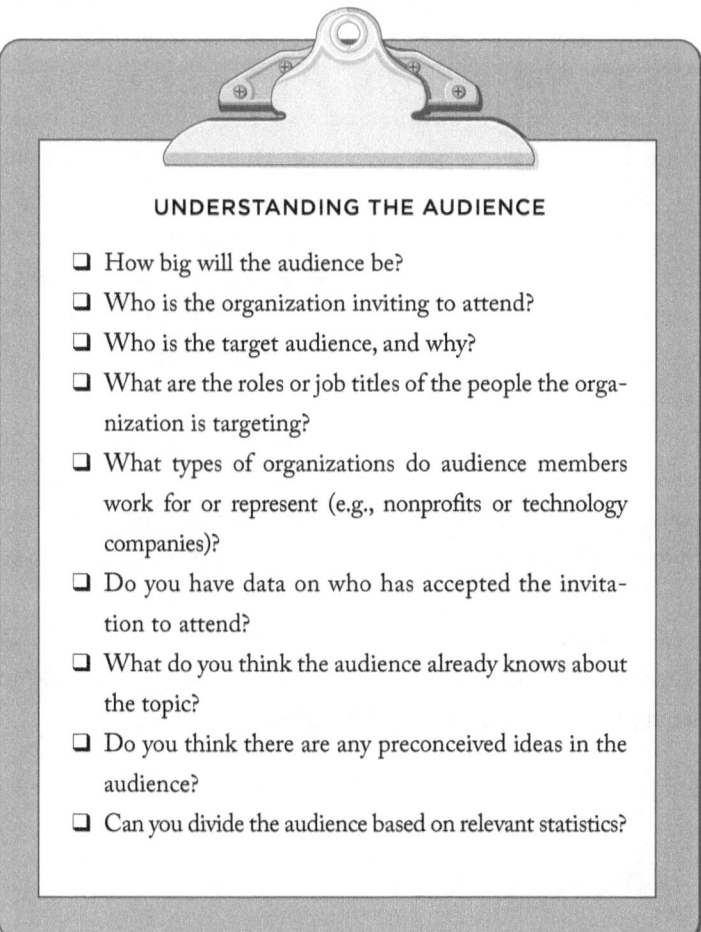

UNDERSTANDING THE AUDIENCE

- ❏ How big will the audience be?
- ❏ Who is the organization inviting to attend?
- ❏ Who is the target audience, and why?
- ❏ What are the roles or job titles of the people the organization is targeting?
- ❏ What types of organizations do audience members work for or represent (e.g., nonprofits or technology companies)?
- ❏ Do you have data on who has accepted the invitation to attend?
- ❏ What do you think the audience already knows about the topic?
- ❏ Do you think there are any preconceived ideas in the audience?
- ❏ Can you divide the audience based on relevant statistics?

RESEARCHING THE TOPIC

Sometimes I've had to come up to speed very quickly on a topic that is not my natural area of expertise, and that's a heavier lift for me in the preparation, but it's so rewarding.

—Deirdre Bolton, Head of Executive Development, Prosek Partners

In-depth knowledge of the topic isn't one of the characteristics listed as a requirement of a great moderator because I don't think it is necessary. However, researching the topic is vital because it improves your presence as a moderator if you know some industry jargon or are aware of recent considerations related to the panel's topic.

Moderators need to be great communicators. They need to take complex information and make it easy to understand. As a result, many moderators are good at bridging the gap between the technical knowledge held by the panelists and the audience's familiarity with the topic. Researching the topic and learning more about it and the panelists will make you a better moderator. There is no need to go overboard—like anything, you could start going down an endless rabbit hole. However, successfully identifying and becoming more up to date on contemporary issues related to the panel topic will be helpful.

According to one moderator, who shall remain anonymous, "One of my worst panels was where I was not knowledgeable on the topic and not engaged with it." Research counts.

5

SELECTING PANELISTS

Putting together a panel is like putting together the pieces of a puzzle. You know the subject, but sometimes you put a piece in place, and it doesn't fit right. You want panelists who don't just give canned answers, but you don't want panelists who are long-winded. It's like Goldilocks—you want it to be just right.
—Katie Flood Ostrander, Managing Director, Deutsche Bank

The worst panels are those where everyone says the same thing, everybody's in agreement, and everybody has the same background and point of view.
—Robert S. Kricheff, Global Strategist and Head of Multi-Asset Credit, Shenkman Capital Management

You could have five brilliant people on the panel; if they're boring, if they're not engaging, it doesn't matter that they're brilliant. No one's listening after five minutes.
—Michael Gatto, Partner, Silver Point Finance and author of *The Credit Investor's Handbook*

"Great chemistry" is how Bloomberg LLP television anchor and moderator Alix Steel described her favorite moderating experience when she moderated a discussion between Michael Bloomberg and Lloyd Blankfein. Having the right panelists can make or break a panel. Sometimes, you might be asked to moderate a panel of preassembled panelists, but sometimes, you are asked to help assemble the panel as a moderator. This chapter is for moderators who have been asked to find panelists and assemble a panel. It provides a helpful guide for conference organizers asked to put together an engaging and thought-provoking panel.

HOW MANY PANELISTS?

Three to four panelists is the sweet spot number.
—Logan Krohn, Business Analyst, McKinsey & Company

The guidelines are flexible regarding how many panelists should sit on a panel. Like many things in life, there is no right or wrong answer to the question of how many panelists are too few or too many. Generally, the "ideal" number of panelists for an hour-long panel is up to four, although no precise science supports these numbers.

One panelist and one moderator is a fireside chat rather than a panel. Although preparing for a fireside chat is necessary, the moderator role is more similar to a journalist conducting an interview than someone moderating a discussion. If you are asked to moderate a fireside chat, you should expect the panelists' answers to each question to be longer. If you have two panelists, it is prudent to determine if the two individuals get along. Although it might be tempting to invite two speakers with divergent views, in that situation, you risk having a panelist storm off stage or you may become the referee between two sparring guests rather than the moderator of a civilized discussion.

The length of the panel is another consideration. If you only have twenty-five minutes, you don't want four panelists because they will only get a short amount of speaking time. If you have one hour for the panel and four panelists, they will each get around thirteen minutes of airtime after introductions and the time it takes for you as a moderator to ask questions. And that thirteen-minute estimate assumes you have little or no audience question-and-answer time.

Five or more panelists are usually too many. If you are facing the problem of abundance, with more than five panelists available to speak on your topic, consider hosting two back-to-back panels and narrowing each panel's topic so you can group three panelists together for each. However, you might need to have five panelists if one of your panelists is not guaranteed to show up. For example, the panelist might be a high-profile figure who cannot commit too far in advance of an event, or maybe they have a history of canceling at the last moment (e.g., at the last minute, congresspersons might be required to stay in session to vote so they can't leave, regardless of the function). Booking five panelists means you still have enough in case of a cancellation. In this situation, I often recruit a "friendly" panelist or someone who understands the situation and knows that if all five panelists turn up, they might get less airtime than the rest to ensure the other panelists walk away happy rather than feeling as though they didn't get to share their opinions fully. Alternatively, if you have five panelists and don't want to drop any, another option is to extend the panel length to ensure each panelist has sufficient airtime to justify their participation.

The exception to this general rule is when the panel is used as a teaser for breakout sessions with the individual panelists. In this situation, having more panelists than the "recommended" number is okay because of the panel's purpose, and as a result, the moderator's role is somewhat different. Rather than solicit information on a topic or further discussion on an issue, the moderator's job is to generate excitement and attendance at the breakout sessions. You want to ask teasers or more provocative questions to draw audience members into the breakout rooms.

Determining how many panelists to include on your panel is something you should thoughtfully consider, but there is no one correct answer. You should use your judgment, consult with the conference organizers, and if possible, discuss with other people you consider great moderators.

IDENTIFYING POTENTIAL PANELISTS

Understanding the panel's purpose is critical to your search for panelists. Identification occurs through a multitude of sources. First, ask the organization sponsoring the panel if they have any suggestions or leads for panelists. Once you have their list, extend the search to include board members (from private companies, nonprofits, and listed corporations) and others considered to be subject matter experts. Universities and advisory boards are other great places to look for knowledgeable panelists. You can also look for an industry association and consult them for recommendations, or you can search the Internet for people who have written papers addressing your topic and are willing to discuss it publicly.

Social media can be a powerful way to find panelists. A well-placed post can often lead to recommendations, connections, and suggestions. Searching LinkedIn and other databases by topic is another way to find speakers. Many LinkedIn members will include in their profile that they are panelists or speakers and the topics they are comfortable discussing. Start with a broad search and then narrow the list from there. Another source of panelists is book authors, and many organizations are happy for the authors to mention their book in the presentation. Before offering, you should check with the conference organizers. A book description could be included in the conference materials to generate interest in the panel.

If you find a potential candidate and ask them to be panelist (which we will discuss later) but they decline, then ask them if they have any recommendations for other panelists. You can also ask panelists who have already agreed to speak if they know any potential candidates. They might have suggestions and connections to other people in the field willing to speak on the record.

As discussed, understanding the audience is essential and can be an important factor in assembling a list of potential panelists for an event. Is the audience limited to the membership of an organization (e.g., CFA society members), or is it open to the public? Are you targeting people in a particular profession (e.g., lawyers) or with a particular skill set (e.g., cybersecurity experts)? Perhaps unsurprising, for some people, there must be "something in it for them" before they agree to panel participation. If the panelist is building a new practice, you might want to highlight how they could reach potential customers based on who you anticipate will be in the audience for the panel. Tell them you expect a strong representation of the target cohort in the audience. You should not exaggerate, but highlighting how this can be a win-win can make all the difference.

You want your panelists to be able to deliver information compellingly. When choosing panelists, look for subject matter experts with some public speaking experience. You can find videos online of speeches they have given or panels in which they have participated previously. You should be able to assess their skill as a speaker and thus have confidence regarding whether they will be an effective spokesperson and panelist.

Look for people who are unscripted. Scripted panelists are the hardest ones to moderate. These panelists don't like to go off script. Unfortunately, CEOs and CFOs of publicly traded companies are usually scripted due to fair disclosure rules. They don't like to talk off-the-cuff. So although you may get a big-name headliner, with a scripted panelist, you risk putting on stage a snoozer who will put the audience to sleep.

One of the rules of panelist identification is ensuring each panelist has contributed significantly to the topic and has something valuable to add to the conversation. If a group of panelists does not meet these criteria, you risk losing the audience and losing credibility. When choosing your panelists, you also need to consider the marketing plan for the panel and how you will attract audience members. Even if your panel is part of a broader event, audience members can choose not to attend.

Start with a broad list of potential candidates. It might be challenging, but you should rank them according to how much you want them on your panel. Ranking your choices will help you prioritize whom to ask first and keep your work focused. If you are looking for a three-person panel and the first three people you ask to participate agree, you're in luck. But if they don't, you need to ask more people. Panelists say no to opportunities for many reasons. They might have a conflict or cannot make the significant time commitment required. They might be in a different city than you expected. It is best if you try to get a recognizable name, or at least one that is recognizable to your audience. This will help you generate buzz and attract audience members.

HOW TO ASK SOMEONE TO BE A PANELIST

Once you have decided which panelists you want to approach, you need to make "the ask." When asking someone to be a panelist, remember you are asking them to take time out of their busy schedule to prepare and attend the panel, and they need to believe they will get something out of it or they are benefiting a great cause. Demonstrating you are a well-prepared moderator will enhance the perception that the panel will go well and the panelist will have a beneficial experience.

There is no one way to approach potential panelists. I have used many ways to reach panelists, including cold calls to their office, connecting through the LinkedIn messenger feature, contacting their executive assistant, emailing them directly, and sending the information to them via post. You can also have a mutual contact send a "connection" email. I have included a sample "ask" email to help guide you.

When you make the ask, you must convey a lot of information verbally or through follow-up correspondence. The first and most crucial information is the date and time of the panel. Many panelists have busy schedules. They might be able to let you know up front if they are busy on the day in question, which gives you both an easy and elegant way to thank one another and allows you to move on quickly and make the next ask. Once you have given them the date and time, let them know if this is a virtual panel, an in-person panel, or a hybrid panel (with a combination of in-person and virtual panelists). If it is in person, tell the potential panelist where the panel is being held. Is it in New York City, which might be a short subway ride for them, or is it in Singapore, which involves a sixteen-hour flight if coming from New York City? As they say, it's all about the location.

Other information you should include is the panel topic and the event's purpose. Knowing the purpose of the event up front is essential. Potential panelists often want to know as much as you do about the panel and its context. You should also be able to tell them if the panel is the whole event or if it is part of a broader conference. When discussing the panel topic, don't just tell them about the topic. Speak to them and find out how their expertise fits within the topic. If they have written a paper about it, reference the paper (and make sure you have read it or have read a summary of it before you make the ask).

Unfortunately, the way to order the list when it comes to asking panelists to participate is similar to a game of chess. You want to ask your strongest panelist first, even if it is a long shot. If they decline, do not get overly worried. You have done the research and are prepared to make your next ask. And the next person you ask to be a panelist might agree and be an outstanding addition.

Some people don't want to share the limelight, and others will assess whether the panel is worth their time and effort based on many factors, including the panel's length and the number of speakers. For some people, it is very difficult to justify participating in an hour-long panel with five panelists (about ten minutes of speaking time after openings and closings) compared with an hour-and-a-half-long panel with just three panelists (with about half an hour of airtime per speaker). If you are unsure of the number of panelists, give them a range, such as "We are targeting between three and five speakers."

Before accepting the opportunity to moderate, you should ask whether the organizers are going to record the event and whether media will be present. This information is helpful not just for you as a moderator but also for the panelists. To a communication native, it might not seem necessary. Still, for many professionals, particularly those subject to their firm's media and communications policy, you need to let the panelists know if the panel will be recorded, to whom the recording will be made available, and whether media will be present. Some firms have strict no-media policies. Others are flexible depending on the event. But it is helpful if you lay this out in advance because you don't want to find yourself without panelists when they turn up at the event and see Fox News in the audience.

People often accept panel invitations for a multitude of reasons. They might have planned to attend the conference already, so sitting on a panel, even if they only expect to have ten minutes of airtime, could enhance their networking opportunities. As mentioned earlier, authors will often accept panel opportunities when they coincide with the publication of a book, particularly if the event relates to the topic they have written about. You cannot assume a panelist will say yes or no based on the number of people on the panel.

SAMPLE PANELIST ASK EMAIL

Dear Ms. Vega,

Please let me introduce myself. My name is Katrina Dudley. I serve on the board of The Children's Village, an organization with a long history of helping children in foster care and youth in juvenile justice and supporting education. Each year, Inwood House, a division of The Children's Village focused on pregnant and parenting teens, hosts a luncheon with a topic addressing something relevant not only to the children and teens we service but also to all children.

Ms. Spence, copied on this email, recommended you as a panelist for our seventeenth annual Inwood House Luncheon. We are looking for four experts to participate. This year, we are focusing on how to talk to our kids about diversity and inclusion. She indicated that you had significant experience speaking about this topic.

The luncheon will be held in person (no virtual participation) in midtown Manhattan at the Yale Club on March 13 from 12 noon until 2 pm, with the panel being the main focus of the event. The luncheon typically draws between 125 and 150 parents, business leaders, community activists, educators, and social workers—women and men united in their passion for changing the social environment for their children and current and future teens. We would be honored to have you participate.

We will not record the event, but we have invited media focusing on nonprofit news and hope they will cover the event and the panel. If you are available on March 13 and would like to participate, I would be pleased to speak with you via phone (555-123-4567) to discuss the event in more detail before you give us a definitive answer.

With kind regards,
Katrina Dudley
Co-Chair, Inwood House Luncheon Committee

THE IMPORTANCE OF PANEL DIVERSITY

My favorite panelist is someone who is really cool, really interesting, representing a different perspective.
—Logan Krohn, Business Analyst, McKinsey & Company

The best panels have diverse voices with strong opinions or points of view on the panel's topic. The best way to have diverse voices is to include panelists that come from diverse backgrounds and have interesting experiences in your panels.

Diversity comes in all shapes and sizes: gender diversity, experiential diversity, age diversity, racial diversity, ethnic diversity, socioeconomic diversity, and educational diversity are a few common examples. When you are assembling a panel, not only do you want diversity of expertise, but you also want to ensure you have other types of diversity. A panel of five white men in their fifties, even if they have the necessary expertise, will not be as relatable to the audience as a panel of a diverse range of experts, including young and old, male and female, and people raised in different countries. We often tend to choose people with years of experience as panel members, which can result in a panel lacking age diversity. Why not consider someone younger as a panelist? They might not have years of experience, but younger people have different experiences that can be valuable and relatable to the audience.

Do you always need diversity? What happens when the panel's purpose is to offer the "female perspective"? Should you only have female panelists? You can argue that you only want females, given the female perspective. But think of the value you can add to a panel of women when you have a male on your panel who is an ally of women and can offer his perspective. You might also include someone who is nonbinary and able to offer that perspective as well.

PRESELECTED PANELISTS

Not all moderators are offered the opportunity to select the panelists on the panel. There are many reasons for this—the panelist might have been chosen because they represent an organizations sponsoring the event, or the panel topic might have been selected because the event organizer wanted a panel that featured a particular speaker.

Review the biographies of each of the panelists, and if possible, see if there is a recording of prior participation on a panel. That will give you the information you need to make a preliminary assessment of how the panelists fit together. If the panel selection appears thoughtful and you can understand why the panelists were selected, there is little else you need to do.

Try to find common ground between the panelists, even if you must do so in an unconventional way. Be creative. If you believe it will be challenging to work with the preassigned panelists, you need to evaluate your options. If you have already accepted the role of moderator, you should be very thoughtful regarding whether you want to withdraw and you should weigh the impact that will have on your future opportunities. You could also work with the event organizers to improve the quality of the panel. You might suggest another panelist, whose addition could make the panel more workable from your perspective. If one of the difficult panelists is from a sponsoring organization, you could ask the sponsoring company to provide another person for the panel. The most difficult option is to politely disinvite a panelist. You should only disinvite a panelist after you have obtained the event organizer's permission. I recommend this conversation be conducted over the phone with a follow-up email rather than by email only. Briefly explain to the panelist why they are being disinvited. Keep it cordial and concise.

DEMANDING PANELISTS

Not all panelists are easy. Some panelists might make unreasonable demands after you have invited them to be a panelist. Although you may be unable to "fire" a demanding panelist, you might want to have a subsequent follow-up call to hear their concerns or demands. If you have already had a prepreparation call with them and talked about their place on the panel, a follow-up call may help you understand more clearly their demands or concerns. For example, they might have felt they were unfairly singled out during a prior panel discussion when somebody took a comment they made out of context. If that is the case, you can assure them you will not raise that particular topic during the panel, repeat the affirmation that it is your job to make them look good, and then offer them the ultimate "out"—tell them that if they are uncomfortable answering a question, they should pivot and speak about a related but more comfortable topic. And remind them again that you won't call them out for shifting to another topic and avoiding the question.

Being forewarned and forearmed is the best way to handle problematic panelists. You will need to manage this person throughout the preparation calls and on the day of the panel. When you have a demanding panelist, the following issues may disrupt your panel:

- Conflict between the panelists (panelist disagreement is okay as long it doesn't escalate into conflict).
- Misunderstandings resulting in panelists answering different questions than asked.
- Defensive reactions to the moderator's questions and audience questions.
- Strained interaction between the panelists.

AVOIDING BORING PANELS

Boring panels happen when everyone agrees. Through your research, you should have identified panelists with divergent opinions. Your research and preparation will meaningfully increase the likelihood you will have an exciting discussion about the topic rather than four people who start their answers with the sentence, "I agree with what the other panelists have said." In those situations, you are looking at a lot of repetitive content and an audience who might fall asleep rather than listen.

There are several things you, as the moderator, can do to reduce the risk of hosting a boring panel:

1. Add another panelist with a competing viewpoint.
2. On the prepanel preparation calls, determine areas where the panelists disagree.
3. Modify the topic to focus on areas where the panelists hold divergent views.

Choosing and composing your panel can be complicated. But the rewards of having spent the time identifying and engaging panelists with the experience and expertise you need and who are complementary to one another are immense.

6

PANEL STRUCTURE AND LOGISTICS

Not all aspects of being a moderator are exciting, and panel structure and logistics are the more mundane parts of your job. But without a panel structure to ensure you achieve your purpose and meet your audience's needs, you are more likely to fail in your mission as moderator.

Thinking through how you want to structure the panel and the day's logistics ahead of time is crucial. It will be much less stressful for you, the organizers, and the panelists if you have thought through the logistics and structure issues before the event rather than on the day of the event.

Different formats create different experiences for the audience. Erin Lyons, Co-Head of CreditSights, recalled that her favorite panel experience was when she and her organization tested a new type of panel at a conference. They hosted a panel of peers who each gave their current views on the market, knowing that the views of the panelists were somewhat divergent. Each panelist gave a longer speech where they provided a summary of their views on the market before switching to a more traditional panel format of moderator questions and panelist answers. They had made the change based on prior feedback, and they hoped the new format would be attractive to the audience. According to Erin, it was "masterful." The audience loved it, and because she knew the topic and had done her research, it was more like an intimate conversation than a panel.

DECIDE ON THE PANEL FORMAT

Panels can take various formats. As a moderator or panel organizer, consider multiple options before you decide how you want to structure your panel. Here are some suggested panel formats:

- *Story-based panel*: In this type of panel, one or more panelists are there to provide their "story," and the other panelists are there to provide an expert opinion regarding the story and other people in a similar situation.

    I recently organized a virtual panel for a nonprofit about the forgotten people of COVID-19 and had a foster parent tell their story to start. It was a powerful way to begin the panel, after which we discussed the topic and the many issues that arose with experts. Those experts could talk about COVID's impact on various underserved populations during the pandemic. Leading off with a story created an environment where other panelists also felt comfortable sharing stories and anecdotes with the audience.
- *Moderator-controlled discussion*: This is an engaged conversation between the moderator and the panelists with questions flowing between panelists, usually grouped around a particular topic.

    A moderator-controlled discussion is akin to a ping-pong game. The moderator asks a question to a specific panelist, they answer the question, and then the focus goes back to the

PANEL STRUCTURE AND LOGISTICS • 69

moderator, who will direct another question to the next panelist. This format is suitable for drawing perspectives from each panelist on a topic. For example, suppose you are showcasing a new product. In that case, you might be looking at gaining the customer's perspective, the salesperson's perspective, and the organizational perspective on how they use the product or its impact on their organization.

- *Sequential panel*: Each panelist in sequence gives a prepared presentation on their views on a particular topic. There is no back and forth. This type of panel is more akin to mini presentations followed by an audience question-and-answer (Q&A) session.

  I have seen sequential panels work well in stock-picking scenarios where a group of portfolio managers give fifteen-minute stock pitches where they discuss their best idea or theme. The presentations are given individually, and then the audience can ask follow-up questions after each of the panelists has presented.

- *Debate panel*: This type of panel works well with controversial topics when you have two or three panelists with divergent views. As a moderator, you must be clear about the ground rules—you can disagree with someone's opinion, but you must do so respectfully. Insulting another panelist will not be tolerated.

  A debate-focused panel feels like a game of "hot potato," with the question being a "hot potato" that each panelist juggles in the air and then passes along to the next panelist. The benefit is that the audience gets to hear various perspectives on the hot-button topic, often from panelists with diverse backgrounds. This panel also highlights the importance of having diversity on your panel.

- *Colloquy panel*: This is a panel where the audience members and the panelists interact with each other. Audience members ask questions and can debate with panelists and make statements about their positions or beliefs on the topic. It takes a skillful moderator to make a panel format like this work because you have to bounce between the panelists and the audience (and you have to control potentially unruly audience members).

- *Academic panel*: Although not a panel format per se, academic panels can be very different than other types of panels, and this can impact how you structure them. Academics have often researched their topics in detail, know a lot about them, and are used to being the solo speaker. In this case, you might structure the panel as follows: speaker talks, audience has Q&A with that speaker, another speaker talks, audience has Q&A with that speaker, and finally, a joint Q&A is held.

I have also found that some academics have difficulty explaining complex topics in easy-to-understand ways and finding those who can is akin to hitting the lottery jackpot. Scarlet Fu, a television anchor, reporter, and experienced moderator from Bloomberg LLP, noted the difficulties of moderating a panel that has professors on it: "They're used to lecturing for an hour straight, not taking a breather, and not listening to others. So, I had to jump in and interrupt him."

If professors responded to every sound or potential interruption in class, they would never finish their lecture. So you need to keep this in mind when you have them on your panel. As a moderator, you must be prepared to jump in and interrupt and bring other panelists into the conversation. It's hard because the professors are experts, but if you don't, they will keep talking.

There is no one right panel structure, and you can combine formats in one session. You can start with a ping-pong Q&A

where you ask specific questions to each panelist and then shift over to a hot-button issue where you get the perspectives of each panelist on the question and allow the panelists to debate the issue among themselves. However, whatever format you choose, you want to keep the audience in mind and ensure the format you choose meets their needs and serves the panel's purpose.

STAGE SETUP

A well-set-up stage is thoughtfully determined ahead of time, considering the structure of the panel, the panelists, and any other relevant considerations. Although the panel may seem a long time away, a prepared moderator determines the stage setup beforehand.

The panel's seating chart must be carefully considered. Where you stand or sit can make a difference to the panel flow. Some moderators prefer to be on the side, but others prefer to be in the middle. Being in the middle works best when you have a panel with an even number of panelists where you can have two people on either side of you. If you have an odd number of panelists, you might prefer to be on one side when you host.

Decide whether you want to sit or stand as a moderator. I have done both, and they work equally well. I prefer that everyone does the same thing; i.e., we all stand or sit. I have also seen panels where each panelist takes a turn standing behind a podium, which some panelists and moderators prefer. But such a format is not great if you have one panelist with a physical disability who cannot stand for an extended period or is a wheelchair user. In this situation, it is better to have everyone sitting, and if you have a panelist who uses a wheelchair, place the chairs for the other panelists to accommodate them.

There is no one right way to order panelists on stage. You can order the panelists based on their years of experience, or if you have a debate, you can group the "for" panelists and the "against" panelists. If you have two panelists who are particularly difficult or argumentative, consider placing them next to one another. It is challenging to confront someone who is sitting next to you. Placing them as such is a great way to diffuse any conflict during the panel. The final way to order panelists is to leave it to chance. In this circumstance, make sure you are the first person on stage so you can seat yourself in your strategically chosen place and then let the panelists fall into place.

For larger panels and when there is a large screen available in the background, I have found that it is effective to have pictures of the panelists with their name and title in the order in which the panelists are seated on stage. This format can be beneficial to audience members who do not know each of the panelists and enables them to ask questions to specific panelists. It is also a time saver, allowing you to dispense with introductions and move right into the panel discussion. Because the audience already has each panelist's biography, dispensing with full introductions does not detract from the panel.

QUESTION NOTECARDS, LIST, OR TABLET

You won't remember all of the questions you want to ask unless you bring them with you on stage. You should make a deliberate choice about the form you use to remember your questions—paper, notecards, or tablets. Some people, myself included, like to have the questions printed on a sheet of paper that they bring on stage with other excerpts from the run of show so they know whether they are maintaining the right pace. This allows the moderator to skip ahead to extra questions without making it obvious they are doing so. I often staple pages together because, if you use looseleaf pages, you must be careful about where you put the pages when you have finished with them. I have often inadvertently mixed pages when they were looseleaf. If you are standing, you will hopefully have a podium where you can place your paper.

Notecards are also an option. Although the advantage of notecards is not having to carry a bulky pad of paper on stage, be careful to maintain an organized stack so you don't reuse any questions. Although it may seem intuitive to place each question you have asked at the back of the pile, it can be dangerous unless you include a card that clearly indicates "The End." I recall one panel when the moderator asked the first question to the panelists again. Instead of ending the panel on a strong note, it made the moderator seem disorganized.

When handheld microphones are used, changing notecards can be difficult or cumbersome. The trick is to find somewhere to place the microphone without creating noise or looking awkward on stage when you are moving from one notecard to the next.

Although it may seem technologically savvy to use your phone or tablet to run the panel on stage, this can have its own challenges. In one instance, partway through the panel, I had my phone go into its lock screen, which was unnerving. (Unfortunately, for security reasons, this is a feature that you cannot disable on many company-issued devices.) If there is a way for you to disable the function, I suggest you do so before relying solely on your phone to moderate the panel.

TECHNOLOGICAL CONSIDERATIONS

If you have ever flown on a plane when there was turbulence, when the captain comes on and says in a calm, cool, and collected voice, "It looks like we're hitting a bit of turbulence," you feel reassured that things are in control. For a moderator, being able to similarly keep your cool, while also having backups in place when the technology goes wrong, is both the high and the low of modern experience.
—Sean Brown, Director, Global Marketing
and Communications, McKinsey & Company

Technology is a factor that can derail any panel presentation. Considering it in advance means you will be prepared if the technology fails. For an experienced moderator, technological problems are the worst, whether using Zoom or in person. It often throws everybody off.

For in-person panels, technology encompasses a range of items, such as the following:

1. Slide presentations
2. Microphones
3. Polling technologies

Slides may be part of your panel presentation. As the moderator, you want to know where the screen with the slides will be relative to the stage. Will it be behind you? Will there be mirror screens throughout the room or just one big screen? You will also want to know how those in charge of the technology want to receive the slide deck. For example, is there a preferred file format? Do you want panelists to email you their slides, bring them on a USB, or upload them to a website?

Microphones are vital because they enable the entire audience to hear everyone. As the moderator, you want to know whether there will be lapel microphones or handheld microphones. If the panelists are seated at a long table, will there be one desktop-mounted microphone per speaker, or will they share? What will you do if the lapel microphone doesn't work? Will handheld microphones be available, and will there be enough of them for all the panelists to have their own or will they have to share?

Although microphones appear simple to use, they can often be more complicated than you think. If you are using lapel microphones, you need to wear clothing that is "lapel microphone friendly." In other words, you need a lapel or something to attach the microphone to. Ties are a terrible choice because they move when you move, so you want a jacket or a button-down shirt to which you can clip the microphone. When attaching a lapel or earpiece microphone, think about where you are sitting and whether there is a side that is the most natural place for the microphone. For example, if you are sitting in the right-hand chair (as the audience sees you) with the panelists to your right, your microphone should be on your right lapel, closest to the panelists, because it is the direction you will turn in when you speak.

New technologies have entered the world of panels. As discussed previously, you can use technology to ask a live audience a polling question. Beware though that the more technology you use, the greater the potential for technology hiccups to occur. Advances in technology also allow hybrid panels where you have one panelist on screen and one or more panelists in person. This format can be challenging, and my experience suggests the most successful way to navigate this is having the on-screen panelists speak first, possibly giving a ten-minute speech, and then having the session move to the in-person guests who participate in a more traditional panel. Toward the end of the panel, the moderator can then go back to the on-screen guest for any reactionary or concluding comments.

LONG PANELS VERSUS SHORT PANELS

There is no standard panel length. Some panels are short (just thirty minutes), and others can extend to ninety minutes or longer. The length of the panel will have an impact on your planning.

A longer panel requires more questions for the panelists, including more backup questions. It can also allow for longer answers to each of the questions and longer panelist introductions because you have the luxury of time. Longer panels also offer the opportunity for more audience questions, and potentially, you can provide the audience with two opportunities to ask questions. I find notecards to be particularly tricky with longer panels because you need more of them, which increases the risk of the cards getting mixed up.

Shorter panels are both easier and harder. First, I have often found that Q&A sessions are cut short or completely cut out in shorter panels. You must also be a much more militant keeper of time for shorter panels because you have fewer opportunities to adjust if someone becomes long-winded. During a shorter panel, you spend a lot more effort trying to get the panelists to relax on stage quickly. This is made even more difficult because you will often cut introductions short to increase the amount of time the panelists have to speak.

VIRTUAL PANELS

Conveying energy in virtual panels is difficult. I stand up. I think that makes a huge difference.
—Jeremy Kohomban, PhD, President and CEO,
The Children's Village, and President, Harlem Dowling

Virtual panels are now common in our post-COVID world due to technological advances and people's comfort with using these new formats. Positively, they often allow access to panelists who might otherwise have said no to participating due to travel and time considerations and the resultant potential scheduling conflicts caused by travel. When preparing for a virtual panel, there are additional considerations for a moderator, and you should discuss these additional items with the panelists. Planning is required for possible connection issues, browser compatibility issues, connection stability, microphone issues, and speaker issues. The best solution is to have a dedicated helpline for panelists. Email is another option, but if the panelist has Internet access problems, email might be unavailable. Before the date of the panel, you should review the process of logging into the webinar, which is extremely important if panelists are unfamiliar with the technology. You should have a technology walk-through session before your panel to ensure panelists have the right technology downloaded ahead of time and can access the panel easily on the day of the event.

Setting the scene is essential in virtual settings. Give your panelists tips about presenting themselves on a virtual panel. Help them frame themselves on the screen and give them feedback so they aren't too close, too far away, too high, or too low. If necessary, ask your panelists to raise their cameras so the camera is at eye level and they are well-framed. They can raise their laptops or cameras using books, boxes, or other items.

Remind the panelists they need to look at the camera during the panel, not at the screen in front of them. Also remind them to keep their cameras on the entire time but mute their speaker when they aren't speaking. Even if you use the spotlight feature, panelists must keep their cameras on because you don't want to switch to a panelist and have the audience see a black screen. You can also speak with your panelists about their lighting to ensure it isn't too bright or dark. The other area you should address is the background they are using. Blurred backgrounds are okay, but often, the background isn't entirely blurred, which can be off-putting. You want panelists to have a neutral background, for example, a bookcase or something similar.

Background noise can distract audiences from the panelist's message. Although it seems obvious, remind panelists to choose a location with minimal background noise and have them mute themselves when they are not speaking. The risk of having panelists mute themselves is that they need to remember to turn the sound on when it is their turn to speak. This risk is more than offset by the risk of side conversations and other distracting noise in the background.

I have found that you need to have more questions for a virtual panel because, in my experience, it is more difficult for a panelist to indicate they want to respond to a question that was asked of another panelist. Another consideration for a virtual panel is how audience questions will be received. Is there a chat feature? Will you have questions emailed to you or a general email account? Should they raise their "virtual" hand? Which method to use depends on the number of audience questions you expect to receive, whether you need to filter the questions (which might be the case if you have a panel with a sensitive topic), and other factors related to the particular virtual panel software you are using.

Interruptions happen more frequently during virtual panels. If there is an interruption while one speaker is talking, try to make it humorous. During a virtual presentation, my puppy entered the bedroom and was curious about what was happening on the screen, so she sat on the bench next to me, popped into the frame, looked at what was happening, and then got back down. The moderator handled it well and said that all audience members and their guests were welcome to listen to the webinar. During the event, you can use phrases such as those that experienced moderator, Sean Brown, Director of Global Marketing and Communications at McKinsey & Company, recommended: "Katrina, it sounds like you might be on mute" and "It seems like we're having a bit of trouble with Katrina's connection. John, we're going to switch to you for a couple of moments while we get that sorted out."

Feedback is the other element missing from virtual panels because the automatic feedback during in-person events is absent when you can't see the audience. Audiences can give you many clues to help improve the quality of your panel in real time because you can watch audience members to see if they are fiddling, frowning, or disengaged. Moderators are rarely able to see audience members in a virtual panel; either they are not visible or they have their cameras turned off. This makes the responsibility of a virtual panel moderator more critical but also makes the job much harder. The following are some tricks for engaging with audience members in a virtual panel:

1. If someone has their name on their screen, use it to call them by name for a question or comment: "I see that Cindy Smith from XYZ Enterprises has joined us today, and she asked an

interesting question during a prior session. Cindy, do you have a question for our current panelists based on your experience as a sales executive in the field?"
2. Use interactive polling techniques to keep the audience engaged.
3. Incorporate audience Q&A earlier, rather than later, in the panel so the audience feels they are being "heard."

Setting up your own virtual panel environment is the final consideration. One moderator of hundreds of virtual panels has multiple screens in his office for these events. One screen has the "run of show" (or sequence of panel events) on it so he knows where they are regarding the flow of the panel, one is the virtual interface so he can see the panelists, and one has the questions on it. If you don't have multiple screens, I recommend printing the questions and the run of show so they are in front of you as you moderate (although it is more challenging to see them on a desk).

Regardless of the many factors to consider in a virtual panel, you can still have a clear, engaging, and successful virtual panel if you take the time to prepare for any unexpected challenges that could derail a virtual event.

7

PANELIST PREPARATION CALLS

The worst panels are when people don't prepare.
—Robert S. Kricheff, Global Strategist and Head of Multi-Asset Credit, Shenkman Capital Management

One of my worst panels occurred despite my persistent efforts because the panelist couldn't find time for a prep call. I prepared the panelist as best as I could over email, but they came to the panel completely unprepared.
—Jeremy Kohomban, PhD, President and CEO, The Children's Village, and President, Harlem Dowling

You have succeeded. You have a panel of incredible speakers, and you are now ready to move on to the next part of the preparation: prepping your panelists for the big event. A reasonable question to ask at this stage is why you, as moderator of the panel, are preparing the panelists. Shouldn't they be doing this themselves? No. Because your panelists are subject matter experts not panel experts, it is your responsibility to get them panel-day ready.

Determining whether a panelist is an extrovert or introvert is key. During the preparation, or prep, call, identifying this trait will help guide you in formulating your questions and the order in which you will ask them. Can this panelist handle a curve ball, or are they afraid of them? This isn't about what makes them a good panelist, but rather, it is about helping you, as moderator, better understand how they operate as a panelist.

Establishing a suitable communications protocol is essential. First, reach out to each panelist and ask them how you should connect with them going forward. Is there an executive assistant or public relations department you should go through in terms of scheduling calls and getting information, or should you reach out to them directly? Do they want to be copied on all correspondence if they give you an alternate contact? Once you have gotten someone to agree to be a panelist, you don't want them to change their mind because you repeatedly contacted them rather than their assistant for information.

Begin researching each of the panelists. Search for any articles or blog posts they have published on the topic or other tangential items. Some of this information you might have compiled as part of your initial research into selecting the panelists, but I recommend going beyond this initial phase. Do a media and Internet search and look at their LinkedIn page. (And while you are reading through their LinkedIn profile, send them a LinkedIn connection request so you can track anything they post using this social media between now and the start of the panel.) If they are a professor at a university, check their profile page on the university website for published articles. Many companies have a page dedicated to their executives that provides good information. Finally, you can often find information about your panelists from profiles posted on the websites of nonprofit organizations where they hold trustee or advisory board positions.

Make sure you are researching the right person. Cross-check information you find on the Internet and through other sources with other information you know to be reliable. I recall approaching someone for a recommendation to a prestigious organization because I had found their name on the membership list. Unfortunately, the person on the list was the ambassador to Singapore not the person I had reached out to! Many people with common names use their middle initial, which is a helpful way to ensure you are researching the right panelist.

INDIVIDUAL PREPANEL PREP CALLS

Individual prep calls take time, but in my opinion, they are an often overlooked and underutilized panel preparation technique. It might seem cumbersome, but it is the best way to prepare. You can schedule these calls for thirty minutes to one hour, depending on your familiarity with the panelist and their work, your familiarity with the topic, and the time constraints of the panelist.

Use these calls to get to know your panelist better. Start these discussions by introducing yourself, the panel's purpose, and the audience the panel is targeting. Ask them to provide you with their background in their own words. They might provide you with content you can use as you develop questions for the panel. Let them know whether they are there to persuade or to inform. Setting expectations in advance will help the panelist as they think about what areas of their expertise are most relevant to the audience and the panel's purpose. It is best if you have already researched the panelist and their expertise, but it is always good to learn from the panelists themselves.

After introductions, ask the panelist to talk to you about what aspects of the topic they are comfortable discussing and why. During these conversations, take notes. Understanding the panelist's "question comfort zone" is a vital part of a successful panel for two reasons: first, it will help you devise the questions you are going to ask the panelists during the panel and ensure the answers they will give will fit with the questions you are asking the other panelists, and second, it can give you backup material.

Backup material does not sound important, but it can be beneficial. I remember moderating a panel of senior investors where one individual gave short answers to questions and would not elaborate on her answers. Because I felt she had not received "fair" airtime, I delved into the extra material I had from our prep call. I asked her, "During our prep call, you talked about Canadian real estate and why you liked the underlying characteristics of the investment you made. I'm an Aussie, and all we talk about is real estate. Can you share your views on the Canadian real estate market?" She smiled, as we both knew she was comfortable speaking about the topic, and answered it thoughtfully. Our audience got additional investing nuggets, and this panelist got extra speaking time. Another strategy that could be used in this situation is to ask two-part questions. Ask the first part of the question, give the panelist the opportunity to provide their "short answer," and then ask the second part, giving them more airtime, even if the answer to the follow-up question is short and concise as well. I have found that some panelists provide shorter answers when they are nervous, so often this problem resolves itself as the panel moves along and the panelist relaxes.

During the prep call, ask the panelist whether there are any issues, topics, or institutions they are uncomfortable discussing. Understanding these sensitive topics will help you when you develop questions. If you have a panelist who is connected to a company in crisis (as a current or former employee, advisor, or board member), they may be unable or hesitant to discuss the crisis. But just because a person was involved in a crisis does not automatically mean they don't want to discuss it. Often, they have learned from such situations and are happy to share that knowledge with the audience. First, however, you need to get their permission to ask them about it.

There should be a two-way flow of information during the prep calls. Take the time to inform the panelist how you will run the panel. How much time will be spent answering prepared questions? For the question-and-answer section will it be a free-for-all where the audience can ask any question directed to any panelist? Knowing this in advance will help panelists prepare. During the prep call, you will have an opportunity to get a sense of how forthcoming your panelist is with information and answers. This will help you when you develop your questions for the panelists.

Create a rapport with the panelist. Find out if you have a mutual interest or if there is a cause or topic they are passionate about. Understanding the character of your panelists will be a factor in the question order. You often want to lead with one of your more forward, less shy panelists, which will give the less comfortable panelists time to warm up. Also, even though someone may be reserved compared to a gregarious personality, they still need to be an interesting panelist. I have directed questions toward more reserved panelists and have been captivated by their answers and their quiet passion for the topic or cause, which they shared with the audience. Being reserved is different from being uninteresting.

During your call, ask each panelist if they need slides. When you have a lot of panelists, slides can be confusing, both to audience members and the other panelists, with the latter often needing help to see them. As a result, I highly discourage panelists from using them. But if they insist on using slides, you should require an advanced copy. You should ensure they bring it in a format the venue can use and require them to email it to you two weeks before the panel date. Also, ask them to bring a backup copy of the slides on a flash drive. Although throughout this book I emphasize making it easy on your panelists, when it comes to slides, the onus is on them to make it work with the technology and the venue.

Don't wait for the panelist to ask about reimbursements for travel. Addressing the issue up front is courteous. It helps if you let the panelist know the communicated policy (the information you received from the conference organizers before you accepted their offer to moderate the panel) regarding hotel accommodations, airfares, and cab or Uber rides to and from the airport, hotel, and conference center.

Request a copy of the panelist's headshot and a professional short biography. Even if you can find one on their corporate website, still ask. The panelist should choose the headshot and the biography for the event. They might want to tailor their experience, highlighting the parts more relevant to the panel and the audience.

Have backup contact information for each panelist. During the prep call, ask them to email it to you or have their assistants do so. Each panelist should provide you with a number to reach them at on the day of the event so that you can check in if something goes wrong. In addition, even though it is in the Speaker Brief, emphasize that it is best if the panelist shows up to the event ahead of time. I typically ask people to arrive at least 30 minutes before the panel. Having your panelists arrive early allows you to attach microphones and make other preparations.

Prepping candidates independently is more work than covering all this ground in the group prep call. But trust me when

I tell you the returns on this time are immense. This solidifies the relationship between you and the panelists, allows them to ask difficult questions in a private setting, and allows the group prep call to be focused more on information relevant to the entire group and not just information relevant to individual panelists.

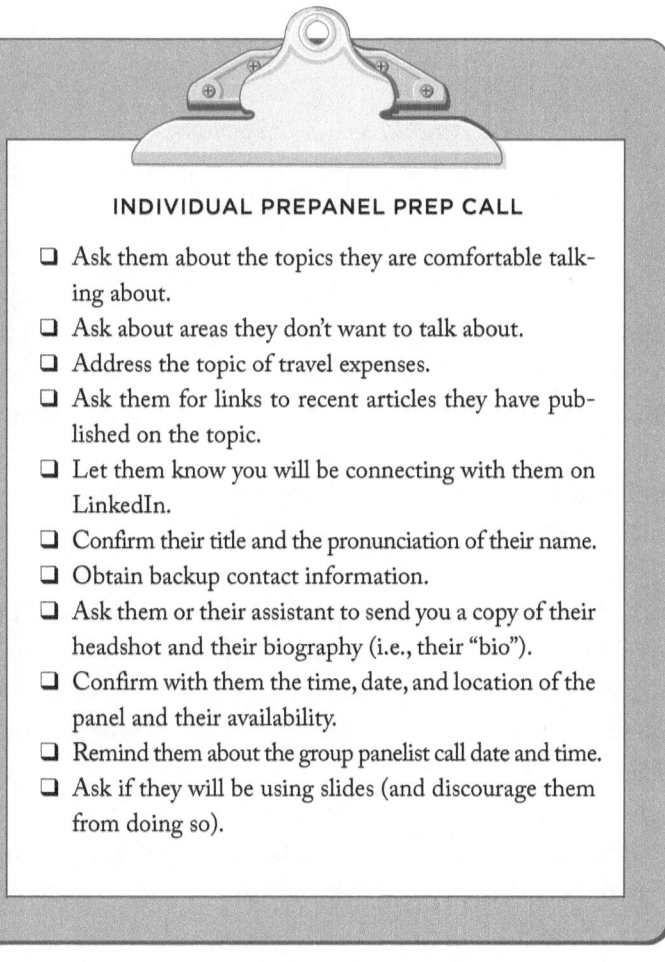

INDIVIDUAL PREPANEL PREP CALL

- ❑ Ask them about the topics they are comfortable talking about.
- ❑ Ask about areas they don't want to talk about.
- ❑ Address the topic of travel expenses.
- ❑ Ask them for links to recent articles they have published on the topic.
- ❑ Let them know you will be connecting with them on LinkedIn.
- ❑ Confirm their title and the pronunciation of their name.
- ❑ Obtain backup contact information.
- ❑ Ask them or their assistant to send you a copy of their headshot and their biography (i.e., their "bio").
- ❑ Confirm with them the time, date, and location of the panel and their availability.
- ❑ Remind them about the group panelist call date and time.
- ❑ Ask if they will be using slides (and discourage them from doing so).

GROUP PREP CALL

One of the goals of the prep session is to develop camaraderie with the panelists. It is not just to talk about the content. You want these people to feel not only comfortable with you as the moderator but, more importantly, with each other in terms of what they're going to say and what they're bringing to the table.
—Sean Brown, Director, Global Marketing and Communications, McKinsey & Company

You absolutely need a prep call.
—Lisa Kaplowitz, Associate Professor, Rutgers Business School and Executive Director of the Rutgers Center for Women in Business

The day of the panel should not be the first time the panelists meet one another. It is important to host a group prepanel prep call so they can at least be familiar with one another beforehand. An introductory call will allow you to introduce the panelists to each other. During the call, have the panelists get familiar with each other, go over the event's logistics, and answer any last-minute questions they might have.

Set expectations for the panel during the group prep call. You should go through the purpose of the panel and the goals you hope to achieve as they relate to the audience and their takeaways from the panel discussion. Once you are on your prep call, have each of the panelists introduce themselves and then introduce yourself. Even though they may already know each other, you don't want to exclude anyone from these introductions.

During the call, walk through the event, the event's purpose, and the panel's purpose. Ask the panelists if they have any questions regarding how they contribute to the event's goals and what they hope the audience learns when the panel is concluded. At this time, walk through your run of show (which is part of the Speaker Brief)—you don't need to do this in detail, but give the panelists an overview of how you expect the event to run. Also, let them know you will be emailing them a Speaker Brief, which contains the run of show as well as other important information about the event and the other panelists.

Remind the panelists that your role as a moderator is to make the panelists look good. I can't emphasize this enough. The panel isn't about *you*. It is about *them*. It is about your *panelists* sharing their experience and expertise with the audience.

Addressing panelists by their correct titles and knowing how to pronounce their names are imperative. During the prep call, ask your panelists what title you should use. Do they want to be called, for example, Allison, Professor Day, Ms. Day, or Professor Allison? Let the panelists choose, and don't worry if there are different ways of addressing each of the panelists. It won't detract from the experience and will highlight your ability to engage with the panelists to make them feel comfortable. By doing this on the group prep call instead of the individual prep calls, you might find that all panelists want you to address them in the same manner, which is helpful. It will also let the other panelists know how to address one another during the event.

By the time of the prep call, you should have a list of questions you plan to ask each panelist. If you have four panelists and five questions each, you have twenty questions, which for a one hour panel translates to approximately two to three minutes for each panelist's response. It is helpful if you let the panelists know this time constraint. You also want to remind the panelists that part of your role as the moderator of the panel is to be the time cop and that, if they repeatedly extend their answers beyond the allotted time (for answers that are two to three minutes in length, the maximum length should be three and a half minutes), you will either have to cut out one of the other questions you intended to ask them or cut their answer short. If you have given a two- to three-minute suggested time limit and one person gives a ten-minute answer, they have taken up almost all of their panel time with their one answer. Such a lengthy answer effectively crowds out others from answering the question and potentially lends a hand in helping you lose the audience's attention, which is a disservice to you, the other panelists, and the audience. It is your job as the moderator to allocate the panel time fairly between the guests, and being a time cop is the only way to do that.

Marketing the panel to potential attendees is not only something the organizers do; it is something you can do as a moderator and something the panelists can do as well. Walk them through this in the prep call, and let them know they will find detailed instructions on how to post about their participation in the event in the Speaker Brief or a separate prepanel marketing email.

Provide the panelists with the "Rules of the Panel," including the previously mentioned time rule. It is all about setting their expectations so they know what to expect on the day of the panel and aren't surprised when you cut them off during an answer to ensure equal airtime. Panel discussion rules that you, the moderator, should communicate to the panelists during the group prep call include the following:

- The only person who can interrupt another person is me, the moderator. There should be no interrupting other panelists,

but if you want to make a rebuttal point, you should please indicate that to me by catching my attention and raising your hand slightly. Keep your rebuttal points to less than a minute.
- Use respectful language when referring to another panelist or their views.
- Please keep to the question posed. Although I will not reprimand you for choosing to answer another question, I will cut your time back but give you additional time on another question.
- I aim to be fair but not equitable.
- The moderator chooses who answers the audience's question, unless the question is clearly directed at one panelist.
- The ordering of panel questions does not reflect seniority. Instead, it aligns with the flow.
- Unless this is a sales-focused panel, there should be no overt product promotions. You can mention the product, but don't make it an advertisement.
- Keep to the time allotted per question. Panelists who go significantly over the time allotted per question will be interrupted, and if they continue talking, they will lose their opportunity to answer other questions assigned to them.
- Jumping in to respond to what another panelist says can be fraught because not everyone is okay with other panelists commenting on their answers.

What should you do if it is impossible to find a time for all the panelists to speak together before the event due to busy schedules, different time zones, or remote locations? If getting all of your panelists on the call is impossible, it is okay if your panelists have an executive assistant, chief of staff, or public relations representative participate in the prep call on their behalf. However, emphasize how important it is for the information to be conveyed to the panelist.

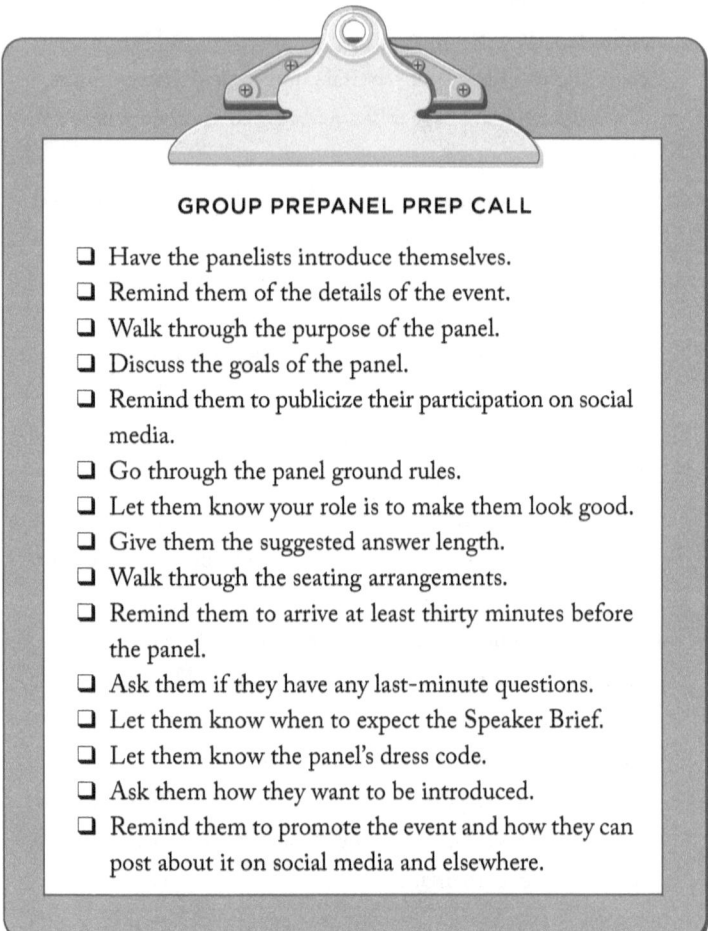

GROUP PREPANEL PREP CALL

- ❏ Have the panelists introduce themselves.
- ❏ Remind them of the details of the event.
- ❏ Walk through the purpose of the panel.
- ❏ Discuss the goals of the panel.
- ❏ Remind them to publicize their participation on social media.
- ❏ Go through the panel ground rules.
- ❏ Let them know your role is to make them look good.
- ❏ Give them the suggested answer length.
- ❏ Walk through the seating arrangements.
- ❏ Remind them to arrive at least thirty minutes before the panel.
- ❏ Ask them if they have any last-minute questions.
- ❏ Let them know when to expect the Speaker Brief.
- ❏ Let them know the panel's dress code.
- ❏ Ask them how they want to be introduced.
- ❏ Remind them to promote the event and how they can post about it on social media and elsewhere.

AFTER THE GROUP PREP CALL

After the group prep call, send the entire panel a follow-up email highlighting the "Rules of the Panel," or ground rules. Your email to the panelists should reiterate pertinent information. Include the date and time of the event, arrival time, security issues, and cell phone number in case they need to reach you. You can share the Speaker Brief at this stage or share it at a later stage.

Reiterating the "Rules of the Panel," even though you went over them in the prep call, is essential because it serves as a reminder to the panelists who have likely not memorized the rules. These ground rules serve many functions. The main one is to set the expectations you have of the panelists. They also remind panelists of the rules regarding what is and is not allowed. These reminders will set everyone up for a great panel experience.

If there is a stand-in for a panelist due to a scheduling issue, you will need to reach out to that panelist separately. Remind the panelist who had a proxy stand in for them on the prep call to speak with that person before the panel. You can always over-accommodate and offer to call them and go through what was discussed on the group prep call.

8

MARKETING THE PANEL

P romoting the panel is the responsibility of everyone involved, from the moderator to the panelists and the sponsoring organization. Everyone involved in the panel wants a large audience. Bigger is better when it comes to audiences. The question "When a tree falls in the forest and no one hears it, does it make a sound?" also applies to panels. If you moderate a panel and no one attends, did it have an impact?

A catchy panel title is critical. Although it might take time to think of one, an engaging panel title can help attract audience members. It is a crucial factor in determining who will choose to attend the panel. A catchy title excites people to learn more about the panel and makes it clear that attending the event is the best way to do so.

Panel descriptions are equally important. An informative panel description highlighting what audience members will learn or gain from attending the panel is another way to increase the size of the panel audience. It can also set the stage and expectations, which means the audience will know what they are going to learn about during the panel and ensure they get what they came for.

The following are some examples of great panel descriptions:

- "After attending this session, participants will be able to identify many different ways to increase revenues and develop more impactful partnerships."
- "Join industry leaders as they explore the latest trends and innovations shaping the finance industry. Learn actionable ways to say ahead."
- "The State of the Industry: What every practitioner needs to know about political trends shaping the healthcare industry."

A panel description can simply include the names of the panelists—particularly if they are well known—or it can include their names and either a short or long title. You might be asking, what is the difference? A short title might be CEO, Microsoft Corporation—it refers to one role the person fulfills. A long title is a multipart descriptor of the person. For example, you might describe someone as a founder, author, and corporate board member. You can also expand your marketing materials to include each panelist's biographical information in promotional materials. However, I only recommend including those parts that speak to their expertise regarding the panel's topic. Create engaging bios because many potential participants evaluate the speakers' backgrounds before deciding whether to attend a panel.

Raising awareness of the panel and promoting it to others are vital to your role as the panel's moderator. Encourage your panelists to promote the panel too. Your panelists are your best panel advocates because they are incentivized to increase audience size because more people will hear their thoughts on the topic. If you plan on asking your panelists to post about the event on social media, make it easy for them. Have a prepared blurb they can use and a link for people to learn more about the event and sign up to attend.

Everyone can highlight their involvement in the panel. Suggest that panelists post about their participation on their LinkedIn page and include links to the panel's registration page. I have seen a company press release highlighting a panel involving one of their executives. You can also use other forms of social media to increase awareness. Finally, nothing beats a personalized invitation. It could be as simple as an email with a request to participate. These invitations, as long as they are personal and not automatically generated, create a lot of goodwill and can attract many potential audience members.

Conference organizers have a lot of experience in this area, and they can help guide you. But if there is no dedicated events team, I have provided a Social Media and Event Promotion Guide that can be used as a template for panelists looking for guidance on increasing awareness of the panel among their social media followers.

SOCIAL MEDIA AND EVENT PROMOTION GUIDE

Title of Panel

Date:	Insert date here
Time:	Insert time here
Contact(s):	Insert the name, title, and contact information of your social media and promotion person(s)

Promotional Links

Event Website:	Insert link here
Event Graphics:	Insert link here
Email:	Insert link here

Promotional Text

On (date), join us at (insert event name), when (insert sponsor) will gather leaders from across the region to discuss strategies to optimize your marketing organization! It's a full day of informational panel discussions and a networking opportunity you will want to take advantage of. (Insert registration link.)

Speaker Promotional Text

On (date), please join me at (insert event name), when (insert sponsor) will gather me and leaders from across the region to discuss strategies to optimize your marketing organization! It's a full day of informational panel discussions and a networking opportunity you will want to take advantage of. (Insert registration link.)

Other Sample Social Media Content

Insert suggested LinkedIn, Facebook, and X (formerly Twitter) content that panelists and their organizations can use in their LinkedIn feeds to promote the event and encourage people to attend.

Follow Us on Social Media

Insert social media links for the sponsoring organization, panelists, and moderators.

CREATIVE MARKETING IDEAS

There are several innovative ways to market a panel, and the technique will depend on the type of event. Here are some of the more original ideas I have seen:

- *Highlighting a single panelist*: One of the most engaging panels I participated in had a tremendous pre-event setup where they sent out an email each week in the weeks before the event highlighting each participating panelist. This strategy was an impressive tactic, and instead of getting lost in potential

attendees' inboxes, it generated new, exciting, and engaged interest in the panelists.
- *Featuring all the panelists*: Another effective technique in promoting a panel is creating a flyer with all of the panelists' names, titles, and headshots. I have often received a panel invitation and opened it up to see the name and face of someone I was keenly interested in hearing from. Having both names and faces can trigger a similar response.
- *Continuing Professional Education (CPE) credit feature*: Your panel might qualify for CPE credit. You will need to check the requirements in advance and ensure you have sent in all the relevant information, but if you can offer CPE credit, you should advertise this fact.
- *Recorded promotion*: Another way to advertise a panel, which requires prior agreement from all the panelists, is to have them record a short segment two minutes or less on why they are doing the panel and are excited about it. In this day and age, you should use multiple media formats to reach your audience, and hearing from the panelists before the panel could attract more audience members.

ADVANCE AUDIENCE POLLING

Audience polling is a great way to engage your audience in the panel. It increases participation and allows for the exchange of information between you, the panel, and the audience. Advance polling of the audience provides another reason to reach out to people who have registered for the panel and a way to promote the event. It can be an effective marketing tool as engaged audience members might invite friends and colleagues to the event.

In addition, polling in advance doesn't prevent you from polling during the event.

Preparation is the key to successful polling. Polling in advance gives you more time to analyze the answers to critical questions and can help as you formulate your questions. Developing relevant polling questions is critical. When developing the questions, think about what topics would interest the audience and use this as the basis of the poll. Keep your questions simple and relevant. You can announce the results at the beginning of the presentation by saying something such as, "Over 60 percent of audience members who responded to our poll before today's panel had no idea what a (insert name of product or concept or product category) was."

Good participation will make the results more impactful. The more audience members participate in the poll, the better and more accurate the results. As a result, you want to limit the number of questions you ask, and when you send the poll out, indicate how it will be used (e.g., to help us develop questions for our panelists) and how long it will take (e.g., less than three minutes to answer three questions).

CREATING USEFUL QR-DRIVEN CONTENT

A good marketing strategy engages the audience in multiple ways. The marketing of the panel and the panelists does not stop as soon as the panelists step onto the stage. Creating quick-response (QR) code–driven content can be a helpful way to leverage the value your panel brings to the audience. We have seen art exhibitions add QR codes to each exhibit to generate pull content rather than push content.

Think creatively. How can you use QR codes throughout the event? You could have posters on the wall with QR codes that link to the individual panelists and provide more background information. You could have QR codes by topic area to provide more information, including white papers and other more detailed resources, the audience can access. This type of information risks getting lost on an event page, and even though it can be listed in a resource section, having direct QR links to a relevant page generates a quicker user experience, more fulfilling audience engagement, and more potential leads for your product or your panelists.

9

PREPARING YOUR QUESTIONS

One of my best skills is coming up with the right questions to ask.
—Ellen Carr, Portfolio Manager, Barksdale & Co.,
and Adjunct Professor at Columbia Business School

A great panel is only as good as the questions you ask. As a moderator, devising and ordering the questions are the most challenging parts. Some panelists will provide a list of questions they are comfortable answering, but that is the exception rather than the norm. Most often, you will need to develop questions based on the event's purpose in conjunction with the information you have learned from your prep calls with each panelist and from reading blogs, publications, and other material they have published.

Panels are known as the lunch buffet of information sharing. Although it is an apt description, good buffets benefit from some ordering of the food into categories that make sense, such as desserts, meat, and appetizers. Similarly, a good panel benefits from ordering as well. The degree of structure, control, and direction the moderator imposes is somewhat style dependent.

Some moderators prefer a highly structured panel. Others are more comfortable with less-structured panels that go off script.

Design your questions to highlight each panelist's expertise. This is why research is important, and if you have an individual prepanel prep call, you should be even more familiar with the topics the panelist is comfortable discussing. Keep questions targeted, on topic, concise, well-worded, and impactful. Put yourself in the shoes of an audience member, and think, "What would I ask this panelist if I was interviewing them about the topic?"

Developing a list of questions is a crucial and complex part of the moderator role. It always takes me longer than expected to develop questions that balance showcasing a breadth of topics without making the audience feel lost. Don't underestimate the time required; personally, I find brainstorming to be beneficial because of the complexity of the task. Do not dismiss any question you think of at this early stage. You can develop your questions by subtopic or by speaker, and both are equally effective. The more time you spend on this part of panel preparation, the more prepared you will feel when you walk on stage and the more likely you will moderate an engaging conversation with the panelists.

HOW MANY QUESTIONS SHOULD YOU PREPARE?

In my experience, most panelists answer questions in two to three minutes. Suppose you have an hour-long panel and four panelists: that translates into five questions per panelist. This assumes there are no audience questions.

The moderator controls the direction and flow of the panel with the questions they ask. Based on your prep call, you should have some idea of the topics the panelist will cover in their answer because you talked about the topic as part of your preparation. Be prepared, however, that the panelist may not stick to the topics you covered in the prep call when answering the question. New information may have arisen or their opinion could have been swayed in the interim.

If you want a panel that moves faster, shorten the suggested answer time by asking more questions. Being an effective timekeeper and cutting panelists off as needed can increase the pace and energy of the panel. This strategy forces your panelists to provide more concise answers, reducing the chance of them veering off track and providing less relevant answers.

The downside of having a highly structured panel is that you lose spontaneity. You potentially also lose the ability to let the panel follow its natural flow. The discussion might start down an exciting path, and the audience may indicate significant interest in pursuing the line of questioning. As the panel's moderator, you will have to make a choice at this point. You could choose to stick to the script and continue with your original list of questions. This is the safest strategy and no one will criticize you for it.

But you could also choose, as moderator, to move into a more open-ended, less structured panel format where you think of questions "on the fly." I find this challenging because there is a high risk of me forgetting to include a panelist when I have deviated from my prepared list of questions. However, this approach is more responsive to audience needs.

Having more questions than you think you need is best. You never know what might come up, and this overpreparation will help you. The panelists might give significantly shorter answers than you anticipated, or they might suddenly decide they can't answer the question being asked. Extra material, themes, and questions go a long way. According to Ellen Carr, an experienced moderator whose quote opened this chapter, "I've never had an unsuccessful panel because I'm prepared, and I sort of go overboard with the number of questions that I have prepared ahead of time." This theme was reiterated by another moderator, Lisa Kaplowitz (Associate Professor of Rutgers Business School and Executive Director of the Rutgers Center for Women in Business), who recommended the following: "Always have more questions than you have time for."

HOW DO YOU DEVELOP A LIST OF QUESTIONS?

There are many sources of ideas for questions. I often review question lists from past panels I have moderated for inspiration. During your prep call with each panelist, you should have asked them to discuss topics they are comfortable discussing. Discussing these topics will form the basis of your questions. Look back through your prep call interview notes and see what topics each of the panelists mentioned.

Put yourself in the shoes of an audience member. Be empathetic and think about what critical questions the audience might have. Consider whether there are different subgroups in the audience who are seeking different learning experiences. Begin the process by developing questions with the audience members in mind.

Read through interviews with the panelists and other experts on the topic. See what questions the journalists asked them during those interviews. Look at magazines and recent blog posts about the topic to see if a potentially topical issue has been debated or analyzed in these articles or online formats.

Generate as many questions as possible based on the interviews. In a follow-up email or, ideally, during the individual panelist prep call, ask your panelists for questions they think would provoke thought and discussion. You can also ask the conference organizers for questions and ideas. They might have suggestions based on other panels or speakers at the events about the issues they believe will resonate with the conference attendees.

Personalize the questions where possible. Keep each panelist's expertise in mind and try to find areas where this expertise align with the panel's purpose. It will help shine the best light on them by allowing them to share their experiences, research, and knowledge with the audience.

The shorter the question, the better, for two reasons. First, long questions tend to illicit long answers, which can cause you to be unable to cover all the material you want. Second, as I mentioned earlier, this panel is about the panelists, not you as the moderator. Keeping the questions brief means the panelists get more airtime.

Some types of questions you can consider for your question list include the following:

- **Questions designed to elicit high-level information on the topic**
  "(The name of the topic) is such a broad topic. What aspects of it do you think are most topical at the moment?"
  "What key trends influence how (insert topic) changes our planet?"
- **Questions that probe and elicit more information about a particular subtopic related to the main panel topic**
  "You mentioned (insert what they said) in a recent article on this topic. Why is it essential for our audience to understand this narrower aspect of the conversation?"

- **Questions inviting panelists to share their experiences**
  "You spent two years studying this population. What are some of the key things you learned from spending dedicated time with them?"
- **Questions soliciting advice**
  "If an anonymous donor suddenly gave you $5 million to solve this problem, how would you spend it?"
  "What are three things our audience members can do to change the rate of decline of (insert topic here)?"
- **Questions where the panelists can share their opinions**
  "You recently published a blog expressing some fairly strong opinions about (insert topic here). Can you share your opinion with the audience?"
  "Not everyone agrees with (insert panelist or person's name). Considering their arguments, why do you think they have made incorrect assumptions regarding this issue?"
- **Questions that showcase how something operates in real life**
  "Many of our audience members viewed the video of (insert name of product), but how does the product perform in the real world?"
- **Questions showcasing the panelist's expertise**
  "Based on your experience, how likely is (insert issue) to cause permanent problems in the future?"
  "One of our panelists believes (insert belief) is the reason, but your research indicates differently. Could you share your thoughts on this issue with us?"
- **Questions regarding the benefits or consequences of caring or not caring about a particular topic**
  "As a society, we have paid little attention to (insert issue). What are the long-term repercussions of this?"

ALLOCATING QUESTIONS

Fair does not mean equal. Although in most cases you will aim to balance the number of questions directed to each panelist, you don't always need to ask the same number of questions to each panelist. If you have one superstar panelist and the remainder are supporting cast, ask the superstar more questions because they have more to add and the audience wants to hear them. Don't go overboard, but it is okay to tip the time scale in their favor.

Why not simply give the superstar a keynote speaking spot? There are a few reasons. First, they may not have enough content. Second, their value might come from having them appear with other panelists with competing views. Finally, in general, conference organizers prefer having panels that feature the voices of many rather than the voice of one.

QUESTION ORDERING

The order in which you ask your questions impacts the panel's flow. A good panel flow increases engagement with the audience. After you have written a list of questions, if you haven't done so already, decide who would be the best panelist to answer each question. Count how many questions you have per panelist and decide whether this reflects how much airtime you want each panelist to have. At this stage, either eliminate some questions for a panelist to whom you were going to ask too many questions, reassign the questions to another panelist if they have the expertise to answer them, or think of more questions. Count the number of questions and divide that by the panel length to determine if you have sufficient time for all the questions.

Asking the same question to multiple panelists works when they have opposing views on the topic. It is a way of engendering debate on the panel in a controlled manner. It is also a good option when the question has multiple answers depending on the individual because it is open-ended, such as "What advice would you give someone starting their career in this industry?" Finally, you can ask the same question to multiple panelists when you limit the answer to just one point: "What is one tip you would give someone who is a first-time panel moderator?"

Repeated questions can be difficult in certain circumstances. Although as a moderator developing the list of questions it is easy to ask the same question to different panelists, if the first person gives a complete answer, this leaves very little additional content for the other panelists. Their only options are to agree with the first panelist or, worse, repeat the same verbiage without adding any real value.

The following are a few rules of thumb when it comes to question ordering. You want to order the questions in a way that is fair to the panelists and maximizes the audience's experience:

- Try to solicit two views on each question.
- Order your questions so each panelist speaks first one time, last once, and in between at least once. You don't want to ask the questions in the same panelist sequence every time.
- I often number each question and then total the question numbers by panelist to ensure the numbers are roughly equal. Checking the question numbering is a great way to ensure you have balanced out the panelists throughout the question session.
- With scenario-based panels, a panelist will often provide a more extended introduction about their specific circumstances. In this case, you should provide a section where you

have panelists answer questions before reincorporating the first panelist into the discussion for their learned experience.
- You may start with questions about the past, move to questions about the present, and follow with questions about the future.

Carefully wording your questions allows the discussion between you and the panelists to flow naturally. The questions should flow from opening questions to transition questions, which go to the heart of the topic, and finally, to sensitive questions. Often, it is helpful to have the moderator clarify unclear answers or briefly summarize what another panelist has said to help reinforce the message and ensure panelists know what has been said immediately before their answer.

TRANSITIONS

As a moderator, it is your job to make the conversation flow, so after a panelist has answered a question, it is critical to have a transition. As you develop your questions, you will need to incorporate these transition sentences that enable you to pivot between the parts of the discussion. Pivoting from one section to the next is an important moderator job and something that you should include in your question list. Sharing short personal experiences as a moderator can make the panel more compelling and engaging. It is also a great way to pivot from one set of questions to the next. For example, if you ask Joe a question about the future of quantum physics, you could add a comment at the end that bridges it back to something one of the other panelists said during the discussion. You could say something like, "Not only do we now have a roadmap for how quantum physics will change our everyday life, but Laila, on our panel, also gave us some great examples of where we should use it today to impact everyday transactions without us even knowing."

THE FIRST QUESTION

Moderators should begin the panel with an opening question. The answer to this question might be slightly longer than recommended, but it will allow each panelist to share their "big picture" view of the topic. Be careful with these types of answers because you want to ensure the panelists don't answer the more specific questions in their opening remarks.

You want your questions to engage both the panelists and the audience. Start with the more accessible topics or a more neutral question and move from there to the more sensitive aspects of the discussion. Consider the first question to be the icebreaker of the discussion, and remember that everyone is likely to be nervous, so try and make sure the question doesn't contain too much content relevant to the remainder of the panel in case a nervous panelist does not answer well.

It is important to start the panel on a strong footing and this includes setting the pace of the panel early. Therefore, you need to be a diligent timekeeper of each panelist's answer to the first question. While you may allow for slightly longer answers to your first question, you might need to interrupt a panelist who becomes long-winded as a way of signaling to them that the expected answer length is shorter than they appear to realize. Failing to cut off a long-winded panelist early in the discussion will likely take away from your panel's effectiveness because you will go deep into very few issues and potentially miss covering other issues. Although some audience members might be fascinated with a monologue about cellular-based biotic robots, you risk losing most of the audience, who might fall asleep or, even worse, get up and leave.

Don't ask open-ended, unfocused questions. In interviews, it is good practice to ask, "Is there anything we have not asked or discussed that you can tell us?" But in panels, that is a minefield you don't want to step into. It opens the floor for one person to grab the microphone and direct the discussion away from your focused list of questions that was designed to address the purpose of your panel and the needs of your audience.

CROWDSOURCING QUESTIONS

You can use a digital platform for crowdsourcing questions during your panel. These questions will often be posted in front of you on a monitor during the panel. Such questions allow you to prioritize the issues the audience wants to hear about. Crowdsourcing questions is a good technique when you have four equal panelists. It does not work well when you have one panelist with "celebrity status" in the field and who is much more well known by the audience than the other panelists. In such a situation, crowdsourcing questions risks having all the questions directed at one panelist, which is against the spirit of panels, where you want to give every panelist an equal and fair opportunity to speak.

Interspersing crowdsourced questions with your questions is a good option but one that takes a very skilled moderator who is good at multitasking. You need to be able to watch a screen while reading questions from your notecards or a piece of paper. You also need to do this while listening to the answers from the panelists on the previous question. Including crowdsourced questions in your panel can make for a highly engaged audience, mainly because the panel addresses what they want to hear. It also allows you to be equitable to the panelists by following a crowdsourced question directed to one or two panelists, with another question from your question bank that you can direct to a different panelist.

DISTRIBUTING QUESTIONS TO PANELISTS IN ADVANCE

There is no fixed rule regarding giving panelists questions in advance. As a moderator, you have the right to decide whether to give the panelists the questions beforehand. Some panelists, particularly those less experienced with the format, may change their minds about participating on the panel if they don't have the questions up front. For them, the questions are akin to a security blanket and provide comfort about appearing onstage in front of a large audience. If not distributing the questions in advance risks losing a panelist or two, the answer should be clear: distribute them.

Some moderators give the questions to the panelists in advance but say they may deviate from them. Another experienced moderator only distributes lead and category questions in advance because they don't want the panelists to overprepare.

If you decide to distribute the questions, remember that you might get feedback on them. If I have decided to distribute the questions beforehand, I include the questions in the Speaker Brief. Although they are in the Brief, I will often send the questions in a separate email because not everyone reads the Speaker Brief from start to finish. I recommend sorting the question list both by the order in which you will ask the question and by panelist. Doing this increases the odds the panelists will review their questions ahead of the panel. You want your panelists to be prepared and focused on the questions you have for them. The more prepared your panelists are for the questions, the better the panel should be.

HAVING PANELISTS CHOOSE THEIR QUESTIONS

If you are unsure what questions to direct to each panelist, have them self-select. For a panel I moderated that discussed each panelist's career trajectory, experience, and advice, I sent the panelists a list of fifteen questions and then asked each panelist to choose four questions they wanted to answer. Often, you will have two panelists who want to answer the same question and that is okay.

The benefit of this type of question allocation is that the panelists are often more comfortable because they have chosen their preferred topic, which usually means they have something exciting to say about it. This also works very well in situations where you cannot have individual prep calls before the event and are limited to one group prep call.

AVOID "GOTCHA" QUESTIONS

Nobody wants to be caught off guard on stage: "gotcha"-type questions do that. Examples of this type of question include loaded questions, those based on faulty premises, nonquestions, "left-field" questions, and personal attacks. Asking someone "Why did you quit your job after one year?" risks having the panelist pivot and answer a different question they are more comfortable answering, decline to answer outright, or get defensive. They might punt the question and say something to the effect of "That's a great question, but I can't comment on the topic," which makes you look as though you are unprepared and don't know your panelists at all.

Controversial topics are part of today's narrative. Panelists are wary of getting on stage if they feel their participation could backfire. As a moderator, you will lose all credibility and respect and, most importantly, you will lose the trust of not only that panelist but all of the panelists if you use "gotcha" questions. Your commitment is to your panelists. It is your role as moderator to make them look good. Asking "gotcha" questions undermines this responsibility.

HAVE SOME FUN FACTS

Having fun facts about the panelists is always helpful. You can intersperse some of these fun anecdotes into your questions. Researching fun facts differs from researching your main questions, but finding fun facts about your panelists is always enjoyable. Ask around, look at their Facebook or Instagram feed, or review prior interviews to see if you can find interesting facts. During your panel prep call, ask the panelists for three fun facts about themselves. This approach differs from having a "gotcha" question where you ask your panelist a surprise question. Fun questions add a bit of light-heartedness to the panel because they are somewhat unexpected and, for that reason, make the questions fun, such as, "If you hadn't chosen a career in the media, what would you do?" Just make sure you don't spring something on them that they are not prepared to answer.

My fun fact is that I'm not just a nonfiction author. I'm a published fiction author as well. People are surprised when they find out, but it makes for a fun icebreaker and is an interesting fact for the audience to learn.

THE LAST QUESTION

Research shows that the last few minutes of an experience are what stays most with people. So you want to end strong! I will often have a surprise final question. It is an excellent way of ending the panel and is usually easy to answer off the top of your head. I will let the audience know it is a surprise. This is the benefit of being the moderator—I get to ask the panelists the final question, although it won't be of the "gotcha" type.

QUESTION TEMPLATE

Below is a sample question template that indicates questions being asked of each panel member. Remember to tell the audience that they will have the opportunity to ask questions later.

- **Samantha:** Can you tell us how you got into this profession? How did you hear about it initially?
- **Anne,** then **Jane:** Why do you think having women in this profession is critical?
- **Georgina:** Why do you love working in this sector?
- **Carol:** We have talked about the importance of mentors and sponsors. Did you have a mentor or a sponsor that helped you in your career?

- **Jane:** You have often described your father as your best mentor. What role has he played in your development as a leader?
- **Samantha,** then **Anne:** The business case for diversity and inclusion has been well documented in many cases more broadly. Can you give your perspective on the value of diversity in this industry?
- **Carol:** Did you receive career coaching? What other resources have been helpful in your career?
- **Jane:** You wrote a white paper discussing why supporting female entrepreneurs is critical. What are the key takeaways from your research?
- **Georgina,** then **Samantha:** What is the best advice you've received during your career?
- **Anne:** What advice would you give to someone considering this profession?
- **Carol:** You've all been successful in your respective careers. Do you think you've "made it"? What is your definition of success?

FINAL FUN QUESTION—All Panelists

10

OPENING SPEECHES AND PANELIST INTRODUCTIONS

You have to set the tone early on.
—Scarlet Fu, Television Anchor and Reporter, Bloomberg LLP

A powerful opening is an impactful way to begin your panel. It sets the scene for the rest of the panel and helps engage your audience. The panel's opening should give your audience a reason to stay in their seats and remain there for the entirety of the panel presentation.

Some panels have opening speeches, and others don't. This is one area where you should take direction from the person organizing the panel. If they don't provide you with any direction, assume you will be the first person on stage. In that case, be prepared to provide a brief introduction to yourself, an engaging opening for the panel, and then the panelists' introductions. Sometimes, there will be a speaker to introduce you as the panel moderator. They will highlight your accomplishments and invite you as the moderator and the panelists to the stage. Some organizers prefer to have everyone seated in advance, at which point the opening speaker exits the stage and hands the panel to the moderator.

Given how many different open sequences exist discuss your opening with the organizers. Will someone separately introduce you or separately introduce you and the panelists, or are they planning on using another opening format? You want to confirm that your preparation matches their thoughts in terms of the cadence of the event. Some organizations combine the panel moderator and the person who gives the opening remarks for the panel into one role, and others don't.

If you are giving an opening speech, write your speech in advance. Do not wing it.

> There is only one person that it has worked for, and it was this guy named Shakespeare. So, if you think you are that good, you can [wing it], but otherwise, write a speech to be spoken.
> —ROBERT S. KRICHEFF, GLOBAL STRATEGIST AND HEAD OF MULTI-ASSET CREDIT, SHENKMAN CAPITAL MANAGEMENT

A smart and engaging opening grabs the attention of your audience. The opening will set the tone for the rest of the panel, so you want to spend time crafting your message, practicing it in advance, and then enthusiastically delivering it. Opening speeches are one area where it pays to rehearse as a moderator. There are many benefits of rehearsing—if you are nervous, rehearsing your opening speech can help calm your nerves on the day of the event.

Brief openings are the best openings. You don't need a long introduction; those take away time from the real experts and make the panel more about you. Your introduction should make a promise to your audience, and the promise is that they will learn something from this panel and that it is worth their time. You can do this in a variety of ways. For example, you could say, "During the next hour, you are going to learn at least three things you can do to help reduce your carbon footprint and help society save the planet we are all destroying." The benefit of this type of introduction is you have reminded the audience of how long the panel will last.

Startling statistics, if you have them, are another excellent way to open a panel discussion. Is there a surprising statistic from your prepanel audience poll that you could use? Opening your panel with a hard-hitting fact can quickly add to your credibility as the moderator and can often help scale the issue for your audience. You want to keep the statistics simple. Otherwise, they may be misinterpreted or construed as dull. Statistics should not have significant qualifiers either. You also risk mixing complicated statistics up, thereby losing your credibility and undermining the impact of the entire panel.

Internet sites can provide the opening lines of speeches that have been used throughout time by famous orators. Here are some thoughts on how to open your panel:

1. If we don't do (insert action), then (insert some dramatic consequence) within seven years.
2. Look to your left; now look to your right. Chances are either you or one of your two audience neighbors has experienced or will experience (insert startling experience) in their lifetime.
3. Imagine a product that could save you (insert the amount of time) each day and all of the things you could accomplish with (insert the number of hours) each week.

INTRODUCING YOUR PANELISTS

It's a good idea to prevent your panelists from introducing themselves, even if they want to. The risks are numerous, including inconsistent introductions, long-winded descriptions of their backgrounds, and a potential to focus on irrelevant qualifications and omit the relevant ones. I prefer moderators to introduce the panelists and describe their backgrounds. The best way is to first introduce each panelist with their name, title, and a brief sentence about their expertise, which is particularly important if their title isn't very descriptive. You will probably get a biography from each of the panelists. If you don't get one (after asking them and their assistant) and they are a public figure, you might need to create your own, or there might be one on a website for a board they are part of (for-profit or nonprofit).

Start from scratch when drafting the introductions. Don't take a published biography and just read it. This never works because something written for reading isn't the same as something written to be spoken. As a panelist, I have experienced moderators start by reading the first paragraph of my bio, and I cringe. I often send over a short bio before the panel but not an edited one. I don't edit it because I think it is the job of a moderator to pull out the parts of my experience that are the most valuable and paramount to the topic at hand. Once, in a fireside chat format, I interrupted the moderator and said, "Let's get to the main event. I'm happy for you to skip my background." I suggested this because I was the final event at the end of a long day and the audience was starting to lose interest. Once he asked me a question and I started answering, I saw the audience sit up straighter in their chairs and reengage in the conversation. Avoiding the reading of my bio was the right thing to do in this situation.

Ensure the introductions of each panelist are approximately the same length. If one introduction is longer than the others, you are showing favoritism up front, which panelists don't want to experience. Also, a lengthy introduction of each panelist risks having your audience disengage at the onset of the panel, and once you have lost them at this point, it is hard to get their attention back. Why create all of this additional work for yourself as a moderator when a diligent and strict editing pen can do the same thing?

Keep the introductions short and relevant. Please don't talk about what someone was doing twenty years ago. Talk about their recent and relevant experience. I do not recommend allowing your panelists to tell the audience about themselves as your opening question. Who doesn't enjoy telling their story? Even if you give the panelists a time limit, say sixty seconds, many will go over because they are nervous. And once the first panelist goes over the time limit, the rest will follow suit. If you have a four-person panel with three-minute introductions, you've just taken up twelve minutes of your discussion time without learning anything related to the panel's purpose. Distribute detailed information about the panelists in advance. The biographies of the panelists should be available on the conference website or in printed materials.

After introducing your panelists, welcome all the participants to the event and thank them for their attendance. It helps if you remind them of the panel's name and title and the discussion's purpose.

SAMPLE OPENING REMARKS

Four out of five girls over seventeen are "unhappy with their body image." If you have a daughter at home, it is more likely than not they don't like the image in the mirror staring back at them. The media's role in promoting unreasonable body images among teens has been in the press recently.

We have three panelists joining me on stage today. Dr. Linda Walker is a child psychologist who has recently published a book, *Teens and Body Image Distortion*, which includes many startling statistics like the one I just quoted about how teens see themselves.

Ms. Stacey Delany has been the editor-in-chief of *Positive Teen Magazine* for fifteen years. It has been a trailblazer, requiring advertisers to use diverse body images when advertising their products in her magazine.

Our final panelist is Professor David Jones of Umbrella University, who recently published a paper analyzing the rise of the selfie and the psychological impact this has had on teens, from increased suicides to unprecedented levels of psychological issues.

Over the next hour, we will look at what parents can do to counter these negative stereotypes and how certain media outlets are embracing a more encompassing view of what beauty is.

To ensure our panelists are not interrupted, please turn your cell phones off or onto silent mode. If you are expecting an urgent call that cannot wait, please ensure you are sitting on a seat at the end of a row, and please only answer your call and begin speaking once you are outside the conference room.

Please do not interrupt the panelists while they are speaking. You will have a chance to ask questions of each panelist at the end of today's panel. We have two roving microphones that will be available at that time.

As a teenager growing up in rural Tennessee, we still looked at magazine images even without social media, but I still liked my body and was proud of it. But today, half of our girls of all ages are unhappy with their appearance. Today we will learn what is the reason for this change in body perception.

THE POWER OF REHEARSAL

All the world's a stage, and most of us are desperately unrehearsed.
—Sean O-Casey, Actor

Practice and rehearsal are two ways to ensure your panel is the best it can be. With busy schedules, you might not be able to rehearse with your panelists ahead of time, but there are several things you can rehearse before the big day. Focus on your introduction, audience welcome, and if you are presenting the panelists, the bio of each panelist. Practice the introductions of each of the panelists and time how long it takes for this segment to determine whether you need to shorten or lengthen the introductions. Practice pronouncing the names and titles of each of the panelists. You don't want to be tripped up by names that are difficult to pronounce.

Practice asking your questions. Saying the questions aloud will help you determine if they are clear or sound somewhat jumbled. Consider recording and playing back the questions. Getting feedback from a peer can also be useful. Ask them to evaluate the questions for clarity, pertinence to the topic, and impact. Ask them to provide you with advice they think will make you a better moderator. Adequate preparation can also minimize referring to notes, allowing a smooth transition to and from questions.

Recording yourself as you rehearse will help you improve. Check yourself to see if you have a lot of "umms" and "ahs" or maybe some "you knows" or "likes." Review the recording to ensure that you are not putting your hands in front of your face when you are speaking and that you are speaking slowly and clearly.

11

SPEAKER BRIEF

A Speaker Brief is a document shared with all participants before the event. It is an all-encompassing guide to the event, covering all the information they need to be prepared for the big day. This document includes logistical information (date, time, and place), as well as the anticipated panel start time and how long each answer should be. The Speaker Brief covers the five Ws of the event: who, what, when, where, and why.

It is an important document shared with panelists, organizers, and others responsible for the event. There isn't universal agreement on what it involves. Some people view it as a document you send out immediately after a speaker has agreed to your invitation to be a panelist to solidify their commitment to the event. I typically send a follow-up email and conduct an individual prep call before sending the Speaker Brief.

PANEL LOGISTICS

Speaker Briefs contain much relevant information. Good speaker briefs include the participants on the panel, the name of the conference organizer, and the moderator's information. In addition to this high-level information, it should contain the biographies of all the panelists and the moderator. More importantly, it contains emergency contact numbers in case of difficulties on the day of the event (e.g., someone can't find the venue, can't find the room, or is running late). For a virtual panel, there should be instructions on who to contact if you have technical difficulties.

Logistic information such as where and when the event is happening should be included. Where the event is happening might be evident to you but not obvious to everyone else. You should include details about the venue and location (potentially including a map if helpful). In this section of the brief, you should also include information such as where the nearest parking garages are located, what the nearest subway stop is (if relevant), and whether there is onsite parking at the conference venue (and whether the panelists need to get their parking stubs validated). The date and time of the event and how far in advance of the start time you want the panelists to arrive should be listed. If it takes ten minutes from when you arrive at the venue to get to the room where the panel will be held, you want to tell your panelist to arrive about thirty minutes before the event, and you should plan on arriving between forty-five minutes and one hour prior. If it is an accessible venue, you could shorten the arrival time to fifteen minutes before the event, although in my opinion, you are cutting it very close.

RUN OF SHOW

The run of show is a part of the Speaker Brief that highlights one of its key objectives. This part of the document includes information on how the panel will flow, including the amount of time allocated to the introduction, the amount of time the panelists will be speaking, and audience question-and-answer time. The run of show included in the Speaker Brief will often be a summarized version of the conference organizers' run of show, but the information and timelines must be identical.

PANEL'S PURPOSE

Each Speaker Brief should highlight the purpose of the panel or why you are hosting the event. When developing the Speaker Brief, you should be attentive to the need to include all the speakers in the conversation. You should also remember you are there to make your panelists look good and that the panelists' goal is to share information that meets the audience's needs. If you have advertised the event as focused on a particular topic, you want to provide as much information on the topic as possible—that's why people are there. If you have worded the questions carefully and ordered them well, the conversation between you and the panelists should flow freely.

POSTPANEL QUESTION TIME

Your Speaker Brief should include a few minutes after the panel as a time when audience members can approach panel members individually. You will need to clear this in advance, but this is an excellent way for interested audience members to interact further with the panelists. For your panelists, it is an excellent way for them to build their network, their brand, and potentially even their business.

INFORMATION TO BE EMAILED TO PANELISTS

Not everything goes into the Speaker Brief, and what is not included can be provided in the accompanying email. The first thing I tell everyone up front in the email is, "Once you arrive, please find me immediately. I will tell you where you need to sit or where to go before the panel. Just before we go onstage for the panel, I will assemble everyone and direct you regarding seating." I will often include some gentle reminders of the panel ground rules, including the following:

1. Keep answers as close to the expected answer length (which is a function of the number of questions and the panel length) as possible. If answers are too short, I might ask you to elaborate on a point or clarify something. If your answers are too long, I will interrupt you, or you will forfeit the ability to answer one of the other questions initially intended for you.
2. We will have audience Q&A after the panel, *or* we will NOT have audience Q&A after the panel.
3. Please do not interrupt the other panelists when they are speaking, regardless of whether you agree or disagree with what they are saying.

Include suggestions on how to be a great panelist. Not everyone on the panel will have read this book or the chapter on being an effective panelist. These reminders will help make your panel engaging, intriguing, and enjoyable. Before sending out these recommendations, remind the panelists it is your role to make them look good and everyone in the audience is there to listen to what they have to say about the topic. It is important the panelists know you are on their side and that if they are successful, the panel will be more successful, which is a win-win for everyone.

SPEAKER BRIEF

Logistics Information

Title of Panel:	The name of the panel.
Date:	Include the day of the week, date, and month.
Panel Time:	Don't forget to state whether it is in the morning or evening.
Arrival Time:	Set this a minimum of thirty minutes before the panel start time. You might also want to mention here how long it takes to navigate the venue and security.
Location:	Include the event location, the room name, and the floor. In this section, you can also include any information that would be good to know, such as whether elevators are located toward the back of the lobby or whether they will need to clear security to get to the room.

(Consider including a map of the location here.)

Conference Website:	Insert conference website if there is one.
Moderator:	Name and title.
Introducer:	Name and title (only if you have one).
Emergency Contact:	This is the emergency contact information in case something happens on the day of the event. It can be a cell phone, an email, or preferably both. Also, this is a situation when two contacts are better than one.

Session Information

Session Objective: The objective of this session is to [insert session objective]. The session objective is very much aligned with the purpose of your panel.

Audience Information: The audience for this event includes [insert audience information]. Provide information that will be useful for the panelists, including demographic information, professional backgrounds, level of assumed knowledge about the topic, etc.

Run of Show

Timing: 4:00–4:05 P.M.: Panel sponsor to provide opening comments.
4:05–4:45 P.M.: Panel discussion.
4:45–5:00 P.M.: Audience Q&A.
5:00–5:30 P.M.: Informal discussions.

Panel Questions

Expected Answer Time: 3 minutes.
If you are providing questions in advance, provide a list of questions in the order in which you intend to ask them with the speaker indicated.

Helpful Publications

This is optional, but you might include publications you refer to during the event, publications that have been highlighted in the promotion of the panel, or publications by the panelists that relate to the topic.

Moderator Biography

Your picture	Your name
	Title
This is helpful for panelists who don't know you.	LinkedIn Website: linkedin.com/in/katrinadudley
	Your biography in one to two paragraphs

Introducer Biography

Picture of the introducer	Introducer's name
	Title
This is helpful for panelists who don't know the introducer.	LinkedIn Website: linkedin.com/in/katrinadudley
	Introducer's biography in one to two paragraphs

Panelist Biographies

Picture of the panelist	Panelist's name
	Title
This is helpful for panelists who don't know each other.	Linked In: linkedin.com/in/katrinadudley
	Panelist's biography in one to two paragraphs

12

ADVICE FOR PANELISTS

Don't be wishy-washy. You don't have to be provocative, but you have to have something interesting to say.
—Scarlet Fu, Television Anchor and Reporter, Bloomberg LLP

The most important thing—they want to do it, period.
—Michael Gatto, Partner, Silver Point Finance and author of *The Credit Investor's Handbook*

Without panelists, there would be no panel. There are many things panelists can do to help them stand out on a panel and get invited back for more of these opportunities. A great panelist comes to the event prepared, takes directions and cues from the moderator, and has interesting content supported by facts and anecdotes.

BENEFITS OF BEING A PANELIST

There are many benefits of being on a panel. First, it highlights your expertise in a particular area to a large group of audience members, the conference organizer, the moderator, and other panelists. Second, it enhances professional credibility, which can help your career. If you are establishing a new business, participating in panels is an excellent form of free advertising for your business. Although you can't overtly advertise it, your new venture should be part of your professional biography that is distributed to audience members.

INDIVIDUAL PREP CALL

Panelists can prepare for their individual prep calls with the moderator. There are things you, as a panelist, should find out from the moderator. If they don't volunteer the information, ask them. If you have a less experienced moderator who hasn't scheduled a call, you should request one. Here are some questions that you can ask during a prep call:

- What is the purpose of the panel?
  Refer back to the list of panel purposes and try to understand if the panel aims to educate, raise money, raise awareness, or a combination thereof.
- How did you choose the panel's topic?
  You want to understand why the conference organizers and moderator have chosen the panel topic and how that relates to the panel's purpose.
- Who will be in the audience, or who are you marketing this event to?
  Asking this will help you think about the degree of technicality you can use in your answers or the types of stories or anecdotes that will be most meaningful for them.

- What areas of my expertise and experience would contribute to the panel?
  You might have more than one area where you could contribute to the panel. You want to discuss this with the moderator and ensure they know all areas of the topic to which you can contribute.

PREPARING CONTENT FOR THE PANEL

Preparation is key. As a panelist, as you prepare what you want to say, you should have some significant points you want to make about the topic and make sure to refer to these key pieces of information throughout your answers. Focus on providing different information for each answer.

Be ready with statistics that will interest the audience and are related to the topic. For example, less than 3 percent of commercial real estate investors are women.[1] Did you know that 52 percent of sea turtles will encounter plastic in their lives, and 22 percent will die?[2] Shocking statistics can help engage the audience in the discussion. They will help reinforce the points you want to make as a speaker and make your contribution to the panel memorable.

---

1. "Less Than 3% of Commercial Real Estate is Owned and Managed by Women," Beck-Reit Commercial Real Estate, https://beckreitcre.com/blog/2022/9/10/2-percent-of-commercial-real-estate-is-owned-and-managed-by-women.
2. "How Much Plastic Does It Take to Kill a Turtle?," CSIRO, https://www.csiro.au/en/research/environmental-impacts/sustainability/Turtles-and-plastic.

The best panelists are engaging and can tell a story to reinforce a point. Storytelling, metaphors, and personal anecdotes can make your message more memorable. Keep your stories and anecdotes focused and to the point. Storytelling is a great way to link your way of thinking or your explanation of something to an object or experience with which your audience is familiar. For example, if you are describing chemical bonding, you could use the following storytelling example:

> As a child I used to make friendship bracelets with my friends. We'd bring over our plastic boxes filled with beads. There were times when I needed a bead to finish my bracelet, and my friend would have an extra one and give it to me. By giving her extra bead to me, it reinforced the power of our friendship, as we were both able to create bracelets that symbolized our connection.
>
> In chemistry, the exchange of beads represents the transfer of electrons. If one friend, called Sodium, has an extra electron, they can donate the electron to their friend, called Chlorine, creating an ionic bond, the same way the missing bead completed the friendship bracelet connecting two friends together.

ANSWERING QUESTIONS

Listen carefully to the other panelists and their answers. If appropriate, either briefly respond to or comment on what they have said when giving your answer. Although acknowledging what another speaker has said is okay, repetition of points is not. While businesspeople say it is great to be a fast follower, panel discussions are more akin to the four-minute mile—you remember who came in first, and nobody remembers second place.

A good moderator will give you a suggested amount of answer time. Moderators are time cops, so respect them and keep your answers within the guidance allotted. If you have two minutes of speaking time allotted, try to keep to that—your answers should be neither too long nor too short. If you give short, closed-ended answers, you risk disrupting the moderator's question cadence because they will need to have a follow-up question for you to ensure you get an equal amount of speaking time on the panel. If they don't have a follow-up question, a short response means you might have given up some of your valuable allotted airtime.

Hopefully, there will be a clock you can see, which will help you time your answers, but if there isn't one, consider having a friend or trusted colleague sit in the front row and give you a one-minute warning and then a thirty-second warning. This will help keep you on time while ensuring you make the key points you want to make.

Directly answer the question. Recall that the role of the moderator is to make you look good, so if one of the questions is something you don't want to answer (for whatever reason), then pivot the question to a topic that matches one of the points you wanted to make during the panel and answer the new question you have posed. For example, if you are on a panel to discuss recent central bank rate hikes and the moderator asks you about the sustainability of technology company earnings (and yes, this is a real-life interview example), learn how to pivot back. In this situation, talk about how it takes many years for a new technology company to generate earnings and how the discount rate matters and then speak to the fact that central bank rates are inputs into determining the correct discount rate. Now that you have bridged, you can launch into your thoughts on the recent central bank rate decision. You have linked the topic to the initial question, are answering what you wanted to speak to, and are showcasing your expertise in this area rather than giving a high-level comment about technology stocks.

If the moderator interrupts you, even if you are in the middle of a sentence, stop speaking as quickly as you can by quickly wrapping up the thought. They have likely done so for a reason, and although you may not agree with their reasons or you might not understand them, remember the moderators are there to ensure the panel meets the needs of the audience members. You might have pivoted to a question they intended to ask later in the panel, or they might want to keep the cadence of the panel moving forward. As a panelist, it is your job to follow their lead.

HANDLING TOUGH QUESTIONS

Several top moderators mentioned that their best panels occurred when they asked tough questions to a panelist. Tough questions sound scary, unpredictable, and frightening. As a panelist, what should you do in such a situation? First, decide if you can and want to answer the question. Second, see if you can pivot and answer another question that is easier for you to answer and that you are more comfortable discussing. Third, dip into your toolkit and challenge yourself to answer a tough question. Lean into your years of experience and find something that you can share on the topic that the audience will find interesting. You might surprise yourself with your answer to the tough question, and I guarantee the moderator and likely the audience will also appreciate it.

DON'T SOUND REHEARSED

Panelists should be well prepared but not too rehearsed in their answers. The panel should be a conversation between experts on a particular topic. Although panelists can have notes with them, they should not read their answers from prepared notes. Some panelists will incorporate data into their answers, and having those data points on a notecard is fine. For example, although I often quote that only 10 percent of portfolio managers are female, the statistics for other industries are more difficult for me to remember. I will often come on stage with some notes about the percentages in other areas, such as the percentage of federal judges who are female (24 percent) and industries where female representation is lower (such as commercial real estate investing, which I think is under 3 percent—but let me refer to my notes and confirm the statistic first because that sounds pretty abysmal).

AVOID BEING OVERLY PROMOTIONAL

Panelists should not turn the panel into a commercial for their business. They are there to add value based on the panel's content. Although you might mention your firm's product or services in passing, keep the number of mentions to a reasonable level. The audience is going to be aware of your company affiliation from the biographies provided, the introduction, or both.

One of the easiest ways to promote your company's product without being overtly promotional is to refer people to a company sales representative. Ideally, you will have someone in the room, or if the conference includes sponsored booths, you can direct audience members there. This leaves the selling of your product to the selling experts and allows you to flourish as a panelist.

SOME POINTERS FOR THE DAY OF THE PANEL

Everyone will be nervous on the day of the event, but don't let that discourage you from being prepared and doing your best. Be kind to yourself. You might make a mistake while you are on stage. But here is some advice—you will probably be the only person who knows it was a mistake, and therefore, you are the only one who will remember it.

Once you arrive, immediately find the moderator or designated conference organizer, and let them know you have arrived. Ask them where they would like you to wait—a green room, a particular table, or an area where you can sit and relax.

Following are some pointers for when you are on the stage:

1. Smile onstage. Remember to smile onstage and look like you are having fun. These nonverbal cues will significantly impact the audience (and the photographs of the event). Think about where you are looking. When the moderator asks you a question, you can look toward them, but when answering it, look at the audience. Make eye contact at multiple points across the room. Don't give your answer to the back wall. Instead, you want to engage with the audience.
2. Project confidence in your voice and answers. You are the authority on the topic, and your voice and confidence in your statements and opinions should reflect it. Slow down your speech, particularly if using a microphone, because your voice will be broadcast. Fast speakers will get muffled.

3. Tell a story if you can. When I recall panelists who had the most memorable impact, it was those who told a story to illustrate their point rather than those who just stated the facts.
4. If the moderator looks stuck, step in and help out. For example, suppose the moderator's microphone stops working. In that case, you can offer to repeat the questions into the microphone before answering them so the audience can hear the question and the panel can keep going as they sort out the issue.
5. Listen to the other panelists when they are answering questions. Do not interrupt the other panelists when they are speaking, regardless of whether you agree or disagree with what they are saying.
6. Eliminate *um*, *ah*, and *you know* from your vocabulary. When asked a question, do not say, "That's a great question." It implies every other question isn't so great.
7. Make sure to get your key points across early. Although you may have the list of questions the moderator intends to ask during the session, only assume they will ask you some of the questions they provided. If you get your main points across during one of the earlier questions, you won't leave the panel feeling unfulfilled, regardless of the direction the panel takes.
8. Be prepared for audience questions and know what questions you are comfortable answering. Do not be afraid to volunteer to answer an audience member's question, but also don't be an audience question hog either and volunteer to answer every question. Even if the audience directs every question to you, see if you can bring in other panelists to answer it. That is the benefit of having listened to their presentations. It is best if you have an idea about their areas of expertise.
9. Show up early and with sufficient time for a sound check. One of the most frequent reasons for poor sound quality during a panel is panelists who arrived too late for a proper sound check.

BRING BUSINESS CARDS

As you prepare for the event, I recommend bringing business cards or cards that provide information about your business. If one of the reasons for sitting on the panel is to make the audience aware of your new endeavor or product, you want participants to be able to find you after the event.

WHEN THINGS DON'T GO AS PLANNED

Sometimes as a panelist, you just need to take a thread and run with it. The panel may not be progressing as you anticipated or prepared for, but staying silent and not contributing is a waste of time for everyone. One trick that I have used is to "pivot." Take something one of the panelists has said and then pivot from their answer to a topic you want to speak about. Rarely will anyone notice, and as long as you are not being a panel time hog, the moderator should give you airtime as part of their need to keep things fair.

CHARACTERISTICS OF GOOD PANELISTS

A great panelist has some level of interesting expertise and an appealing personality. There are a lot of characteristics that make a great panelist, and great moderators have shared some common ingredients with me over the years as to which characteristics make them want to extend a repeat invitation to a panelist.

    A great panelist has domain expertise and knowledge, and they are open to having a conversation. The audience is there to hear their perspective and learn from their experience. Be excited to answer the moderator's questions and provide a deep dive into the topic based on your experience. The enthusiasm displayed by an engaged panelist is contagious, so let it shine through.

Be willing to participate in the discussion and do not become defensive. Respond to other panelists' points, but don't simply agree or reiterate them. Don't be afraid of standing up for your point of view or debating with other panelists. Use your voice to convey your message, but understand how your answer plays into the overall discussion. A great panelist brings candor and has a clear point of view that is meaningful. Bring some statistics and data to support your speaking points, but more importantly, bring your stories and anecdotes. People want to hear them.

CHARACTERISTICS OF BAD PANELISTS

"Bad moms" in a movie might be funny, but bad panelists are not. Based on many conversations with experienced moderators, here are some characteristics that, if you display them, will pretty much guarantee you don't get invited back.

A bad panelist is unable to respond to cues, such as keeping their answers within the suggested time for each answer. Debate is encouraged, but defensiveness is not. A boring panelist is another warning sign—bad panelists are disengaged and lack energy and excitement. They might be there because they were "forced" to be, but that doesn't excuse a bad attitude. Worse still, they share their advice, not their stories.

One last characteristic of a terrible panelist is when the panelist is two-handed. Yes, most of us have two hands, but in a panel format, they are the ones that say, on the one hand, this, and on the other hand, that. Take a stand, have an opinion or stance on a topic, and don't appear indecisive or on the fence.

13

ADVICE FOR ORGANIZERS

As event organizers, you have hosted many successful panels. The following are ways to help you select better moderators and, once selected, to partner with them to make the panel more impactful for your audience.

CHOOSE YOUR MODERATOR WISELY

One of the biggest decisions that an organizer will make that will determine the panel's success is their choice of moderator. A good moderator has two roles: the first is to make the panelists look good, and the second is as an advocate for the audience.

Organizers should consider a moderator's skills, experiences, personal characteristics, and communication style in the selection process. The list of characteristics, provided earlier in this book, that make for a good moderator is not comprehensive. More importantly, a moderator doesn't need to possess all of these characteristics to be a great moderator. Some of these characteristics may come more easily to some people—such as being a good actor—others may not.

BE CLEAR ON THE PANEL'S PURPOSE

The most important question to answer when planning a panel is, "Why are we doing this panel?" There are many different reasons to hold a panel, from educational to promotional. As an organizer, you need to determine the purpose, communicate it to the panelists and the moderator, and make sure the topic of the panel aligns with the purpose.

SET EXPECTATIONS

The best panels are those where the moderator has clear expectations of what they should do. As an event organizer, you should stress the importance of preparation and how the commitment to moderate extends beyond the panel itself. Offer assistance to moderators in setting up individual and group prep calls and partner with them to help market the panel.

The most important document is the Speaker Brief, including the run of show, and you should help your moderator draft it and provide as much information as you can. If the moderator hasn't seen a Speaker Brief before, provide them with a sample from a prior event. A good run of show and a great Speaker Brief will elevate your panel before you've even stepped on stage.

PICKING THE PANELISTS

As an event organizer, you have the option to pick the panelists in advance of selecting the moderator. Having preselected panelists reduces the amount of work for the moderator. The risk is that it may make it more difficult to recruit a moderator, particularly if one of the panelists is controversial. Involving your moderator in the panel selection process will give them an opportunity to shape the panel, increasing their engagement.

PANEL TOPIC

When choosing the topic for your panel, you should start with a broad topic and narrow it. Having a topic that is too broad is likely to attract generalists rather than specialists in the field, who are more drawn to narrower and focused discussions. Work with the moderator to narrow a broad panel topic based on the panelists you recruit.

ALLOCATING APPROPRIATE TIME FOR THE PANEL

Event organizers control the event schedule, which includes the time allocated to each panel. The moderator then works within the allotted time to ensure they have the right number of guests and the right number of questions. Consider the importance of the topic, the purpose of the panel, and how this panel fits into the overall event structure.

Short panels are usually faster paced, but they come at the expense of more changeover time. Longer panels allow for deeper discussion on the issue with the risk that you could lose the audience if the speakers are not engagement or give long-winded answers. If you have preselected the panelists, the number of panelists will influence the amount of time allocated to each. The more panelists, the longer the panel should be.

MAKE TECHNOLOGY AVAILABLE

There are so many new technologies that are available to make panels more engaging. As an event organizer, you should make your moderator aware of technology that will be available to them before and during the event. From polling technology to QR codes and on-stage screens, let them know their options in advance.

Before the event, let the moderator know what type of microphones will be used for the panelists and whether the audience will have standing or roaming microphones for questions. Let the moderator know about the seating options available on stage and whether there will be a lectern for opening speeches.

Finally, tell the moderator if you plan to have someone introduce them and/or the panelists or if you expect the moderator to take care of all introductions. If you have chosen someone who will provide a short opening address before the panel, advise the moderator and connect the two people in advance of the panel.

SHARE DATA AND INFORMATION

Have audience data and statistics readily available for moderators so they have a better understanding of who will be in the audience. This will help the moderator tailor the panel's questions and content. Are the attendees early in their career, mid-career, or a mix of both? Are they senior executives only? Any information you can provide will be helpful.

Although you might be reluctant to disclose sponsorship information, you should consider it. For example, if the conference is sponsored by Coca-Cola, your moderator might want to know that so that when they are recruiting panelists, they can avoid Pepsi employees. It will also give the moderator some guardrails regarding their content. Solicit the moderator's opinion and involve them in these decisions. In the case of Coca-Cola, you might conclude that a panel about obesity is off-limits; however, they might want to tackle the issue head on and use the panel as an opportunity to educate the audience and potentially refute the link between soft drink consumption and obesity.

TRAVEL REIMBURSEMENT

Some moderators are hesitant to ask about expense reimbursement, so as an experienced event organizer, if the moderator doesn't ask, you should clearly communicate your policy with them in advance. This includes payment for transportation to and from the event, hotel accommodation, and flights. It is better for people to know the expense reimbursement policy in advance, rather than have their expenses denied after.

FIRST-TIME MODERATORS

Every moderator needs their first opportunity. We have already highlighted the many career benefits of being a moderator, from showcasing leadership skills to building executive presence. Within any event, there are some panels that are less important than others. If you have such a panel, consider offering the moderator role to a first-time moderator. Provide them with guidance and advice (and yes, even a copy of this book). Not only will you be giving someone an opportunity to shine, but you will also be expanding your roster of moderators that you can call upon for future events.

14

PREPANEL DAY PEP TALK

A moderator walks a difficult tightrope between candidness and being prepared and scripted.
—Katie Flood Ostrander, Managing Director, Deutsche Bank

Be natural and in your own style so the audience sees you as a real person.
—Alix Steel, Television Anchor, Bloomberg LLP

You have a very powerful voice, and you should use it more when you moderate.
—Jeremy Kohomban, PhD, President and CEO,
The Children's Village, and President, Harlem Dowling

Here is your panel day pep talk. You want to review this chapter *before* the event but not too far in advance. You want this advice to stay with you throughout the panel. You should make a list of reminders to help you on the day of the event.

Be excited and look forward to the panel. Being a moderator is your chance to shine, and you have done all the preparation ahead of time, so now it is time to bring all that hard work together and show the audience what you and your panel have prepared for them.

I will often put a box at the top of my question sheet with words such as the following:

Smile	Sit Up Straight	Speak Slowly
Tell Stories	Don't Get Emotional	
THREE-MINUTE ANSWERS	AUDIENCE Q&A AT END	CLOSEOUT

The list is a reminder of all the things that I want to make sure I'm doing during the panel. The above list is my own. Your list can be, and probably should be, different. As an example, if you use many filler words or rely on one phrase, you could put "No *you knows*" on the list to remind yourself not to inject those two words into your questions.

Remember that even though you've done a lot of work ahead of time, prepped for the panel, and distributed your questions in advance (if that is what you decided to do), now is not the time to relax and take a break. Although you won't be providing answers, prior knowledge of the topic will help you engage more with the panelists and facilitate transitions between panelists and questions, which helps make the panel flow.

BE TRUE TO YOUR MODERATOR STYLE

A great moderator is one who owns their style and is comfortable with their authentic style.
—Nicole Valentine, FinTech Director, Milken Institute

Developing your moderator style is similar to finding your voice. You will get there, although it might take a few tries to see what style fits you best and whether a single style or a combination of styles better suits you as a moderator. Although you might deeply respect a particular moderator, they might have a style that is different from yours. If you try to imitate their style, you will lose your voice and potentially come across as inauthentic.

Because different moderators have different styles, there is no "right" or "wrong" style, but it is better to consider the various styles and find one that aligns with your personality. Developing a personal style takes time, just like it took you time to develop your dress style. You might also need to try on a few styles before you find the right fit. Some moderators prefer a more formal style of questioning, which works for them. For panels that are scientific or focused on technical topics, this type of style works remarkably well. Other moderators are empathetic and can put themselves in the panelists' shoes. This style is particularly relevant for social service panels where the panelists share their stories and knowledge from their experiences. Having an empathic moderator can be very reassuring and help nervous panelists relax. Humorous moderators use light humor to engage the panelists and the audience. An eager learner, as the name suggests, is a moderator eager to learn as much as possible during the panel, and they share their excitement for learning with the panelists and the audience.

Effective moderating weaves together a complex set of skills. Each moderator brings richness and uniqueness to the experience. Your unique skills and experiences will emerge throughout moderating the panel, particularly as you develop your moderating style and let it shine through. Moderating a panel is cognitively and emotionally demanding. You are onstage. All lights are on you, and you are trying to manage a diverse group of personalities to orchestrate an experience that gives maximum value to the audience.

A good moderator will have high regard for the panelists, understanding that each panelist has a unique vision that will contribute to the discussion. Regardless of your moderator style, this must permeate the entire experience for the panelists—from the first time you speak with them to the closing thank you for their participation. Your panelists' opinions may differ from yours, but you should never show that. Your panelists are giving you their time, their expertise, their stories, and their contacts—you should be grateful for this.

MODERATOR PRESENCE

Tune in, ask questions, and just stay super engaged.
—Katie Flood Ostrander, Managing Director, Deutsche Bank

Moderator presence is something that transcends your moderator style. Moderator presence will give you the gravitas to fully command your panelists, engage with them, be charismatic, and lead them through the conversation. You will also need to show the panelists some tough love when they are deviating off topic or giving long-winded answers. Do this well by sharing your leadership presence and in a way that doesn't result in the panelists becoming disengaged and defensive.

Be focused on your discussion. Your panel should focus on a single idea or a single topic. You want to ensure the panelists answer using familiar concepts the audience understands. As the moderator, you have a role to play in clarifying things and making the content accessible to the audience members. A panel that goes completely over the audience's heads will not be of value to anyone—audience members, you, or the panelists themselves.

Vivid explanations engage audiences, and if you start to use them, your panelists might follow your lead. In your questions, use clear and crisp examples to help your audience understand the topic better. You don't want to use dry scientific terminology, and you don't want panelists to include such terms in their answers. Answers are not supposed to be a lullaby that sends your audience to sleep.

Certain words are more engaging than others, and you should work on including them in your dialogue. Instead of just talking about the benefit of something, engage the audience with exciting, interesting, and informative words. Highlight how the views are new or whether there has been a pivot in thinking about a topic or issue. Don't simply use the word "change," which is not very exciting. Unexpected, odd, and unusual descriptors can make concepts come to life. A "plethora" of examples abound, including luminous and, my favorite, phantasmagorical.

ELIMINATE FILLER WORDS AND PHRASES

Filler words are short, meaningless words. They are the fastest way for moderators (and any speaker, for that matter) to lose credibility with the audience. Avoiding overuse of filler words and phrases isn't just useful for the panel. It is good advice regardless of where you are speaking.

Filler words include the following:

- You know
- Umm
- Err
- Ah
- Like
- Okay
- Well
- Totally
- I'm sorry

- I think
- You see
- Literally
- Right
- Very
- Basically
- Look
- No offense
- Actually

Even worse than filler words are filler phrases, such as the following:

- "So, you know..."
- "For what it's worth..."
- "Needless to say..."
- "I'm asked that a lot."
- "I know just how you feel."
- "As I previously stated..."
- "This may sound stupid..."
- "If I were you..."
- "To be honest..."
- "Let me think."

This is not a comprehensive list. You could add many more phrases and words, but as you can see, many of these words are superfluous and don't add meaning to the answer or the question. How do you identify potential filler words? Think about what would happen if you were to run your answer through Grammarly. These are the words and phrases it would eliminate for conciseness. You should aim to treat them similarly.

LEARN TO SUMMARIZE WELL

A panel is merely a presentation split among several speakers. That means that as a moderator, you need to bring all the components to a conclusion for the audience. Keep a piece of notepaper and a pen handy to make notes. It will make it easier for you to summarize the panelists' key points at the end and give an effective conclusion to the panel.

Throughout the panel, you might also need to summarize specific panelists' answers. People often like to do what we call an "information dump." Suppose one of your panelists, who is particularly nervous, does this. You cannot interrupt them, especially if they are within their allotted time. But you can help improve their answer by summarizing the one or two key points the panelist made to ensure the audience takes away those critical points from the panel.

HAVE FUN AND INVOKE WONDER

The best part is when everybody wants to be there; they are really enthusiastic and they want to not just answer the question, they want to share an anecdote or personal experience.
—Joyce Chang, Managing Director and Chair, Global Research JPMorgan

All work and no play make for a dull panel. This doesn't mean you need to be a humorous moderator or comedian, but you should show you enjoy learning and are enjoying the experience. Your audience will feel excited about the topic, the panelists, and the event.

Chris Anderson, the curator of TED Talks, suggests using curiosity to engage. He also recommends that TED Talk speakers ask a rhetorical question. As a moderator, try to spark a desire in the audience's minds to learn about the topic in a new way. You want to invoke wonder in your audience. You want the audience to be as excited as you are to learn more about the panel's topic. If you can arouse curiosity, you will draw more of the audience in, making them want to learn more. In the panel context, this means they will pay attention longer. You want to provoke their interest and spark curiosity. This can happen if the panel topic is something new, but it can also be as simple as providing a new data point the audience is unaware of or a startling statistic in your introduction.

Stir the curiosity of your audience. Talk about something you know that the audience does not, such as a piece of information or knowledge about an event. Regardless of what the information is, when people think you know something they don't, they become curious. Hinting at the panel's conclusion is another way to invoke curiosity. You could also promise the audience a benefit if they listen to the entire panel. For example, "If you listen today, you will find at least three ways to help keep your teenager off social media and engaged in discussions at the dinner table." You could ask a question, such as "Would you prefer to . . . ?" Or you could paint a picture using a statement beginning, "Imagine a world in which . . ."

To help the panel be informative regarding a new product, you could hold the product or use the product in a new and engaging way. You could also tell a story (keep it brief because you are the moderator) about the product and how it changed and improved your daily routine. Remember Steve Jobs's famous speech before unveiling the iPhone for the first time? He generated curiosity, and everyone stayed around and listened to what he had to say and remembered it.

THE POWER OF STORYTELLING

A story can be powerful and a great way to start a panel or for a panel member to answer a question: "Imagine a world in which gender is not an identifier on your job applications, and people are hired based on their talent, not on gender. Well, our panelists have some great ideas of how to achieve this."

Storytelling is a very effective means of communication. It often results in the storyteller's and the listener's brains syncing.

It makes your panelists relatable to the audience and engages them in the discussion. Stories also grab your audience's attention, so you might want to save your stories for the middle of the discussion to reengage the audience if they have started to drift off during the discussion.

As a moderator, consider sharing a short personal anecdote, but let me emphasize the word *short*. As a moderator, you shouldn't be focusing on you. Focus on the panelists and have them share their stories with the audience. However, if you tell a short anecdote, others will feel free to do so, too. Your panelists should feel free to share a personal anecdote when answering a question. Maybe they will share a story of why they got into a particular area, such as their niece was diagnosed with cystic fibrosis and inspired them to research a cure in this area or to start a foundation that raises money for research.

> You should be able to share something as small as your personal experience within the question because it makes it more of a dialogue versus an interrogation.
> —NICOLE VALENTINE, FINTECH DIRECTOR, MILKEN INSTITUTE

> I really like storytelling and with a panel you are weaving together different experiences, like a story.
> —SHARI KRULL, CHIEF EXECUTIVE OFFICER, STREETWISE PARTNERS

Ask your panelists to share their vulnerabilities. Brene Brown makes this point in a TED Talk about how sharing vulnerability builds delight, trust, and loyalty. Having your panelist share their learning experiences and the mistakes they might have made makes them more relatable and engaging. Brene Brown once said, "Storytelling is just research with a soul." I agree.

EMOTIONS AND BODY LANGUAGE

Your posture on stage sends a message. Body language says a lot. A moderator's body language provides cues for everyone, from the panelists to the audience. If you appear laid back and casual, the panelists will, too. If you are slouching, it's unlikely your panelists will all be sitting up straight. Your body language should convey your excitement about the topic and for being the moderator. You should sit forward in your seat and be engaged. You should also remain engaged throughout the panel. You can't simply ask a question and then check out of the discussion altogether. At the same time, I will admit that when moderating a panel, I can be distracted by a late audience member entrance, and I might not hear everything a panelist says, so I do try to make sure I pay attention despite the distractions. One of the best ways to ensure you pay attention is to keep a notebook or a piece of paper and write things down as people speak. Writing things down will remind you of areas you want to follow up on.

Emotional control is paramount. During the panel, you, as the moderator, must exhibit control of your emotions. You cannot let your emotions take over, regardless of what one of the panelists has said. You might disagree with their answer, but you cannot shake your head or say "no" when they are responding. They have rights, which includes the right to their own opinion. During a panel, you must consider yourself a neutral party in the discussion. Although you can comment on a particular panelist's answer to your question with phrases such as "I understand that" or "That was an interesting point," you can't say things such as "I agree with David" because it might put you in a position of disagreeing with another panel member. The only time it is okay to react as a moderator is when someone tells a sad story or, if you have allowed them to, shows a video, and it makes you cry. Crying is the one emotion that is impossible to control.

SPEAK SLOWLY

The world is becoming increasingly diverse, and there is a strong chance you will have someone in your audience for whom the panel's language is not their first language. Speak slowly! It will also help if you have a microphone. I know it is hard, but as you prepare to go on stage, think about how you can slow down your speech. Remind yourself to keep your question pace measured. If there is an echo in the room, speaking slowly will help the panelists because it will ensure they understand the question you are asking and can answer the question, rather than some other question they thought you asked. That's a win-win all around.

LEARNING PRONUNCIATION AND TITLES

There is no excuse for not pronouncing someone's name correctly. It is acceptable for you to ask your panelists how to pronounce their names. After you have done this, write it down phonetically so when you have to say it at the event *you get it right*. Nothing is more unsettling to a panelist than being called by an incorrect name because the moderator (i.e., you) mispronounced it. Also, check whether they prefer to be referred to by their first name, middle name, or both. And make sure you have their correct title, do they prefer to be called doctor, Ms. or Mrs? Do they prefer you omit titles altogether?

You should also know common jargon used in the field related to the panel's topic and how to pronounce those words. Do a little digging before your panel, listen carefully on your prep calls, note down any terms you think are particularly difficult, and then phonetically spell them out. It will help you look much brighter on the day of the panel if you pronounce key terms correctly. There are many programs online that you can use to learn to pronounce words, so you can use those as a backup if you don't know how to pronounce a term you come across in your research. Additionally, with industry jargon, explain the term if you think the audience won't understand it.

HANDLING THE STAR PANELIST

You might have a star panelist, and as a moderator, it can be enormously intimidating. But you need to engage with them as equals, even if you are faking it. If you can speak to them ahead of the event, talk to them like you'd talk to a friend—ask them about their hobbies and their favorite food. Avoid talking about their favorite vacation spot—it might be difficult for you to relate to.

People can easily tell if you are intimidated by them, so you need to fake it until you make it. Create an environment where you are equals—an "equal feeling space." Someone told me just before I was to meet with a billionaire CEO to remember that he puts his pants on the same way as I do—one leg at a time. It was a great reminder that even though their bank accounts have more zeros or they have millions of Twitter followers, they are still just people.

15

THE DAY OF THE PANEL

There's much more anxiety being a moderator than being a panelist as the moderator doesn't have a backup as the panelists do.
—Ellen Carr, Portfolio Manager, Barksdale & Co., and Adjunct Professor at Columbia Business School

It's a lot of pressure when you're moderating a panel; you are reading your panelists, you're reading the room, you're managing time restrictions, and Q&A. There's a lot happening at once, which I think is also very exciting, but it can be challenging.
—Shari Krull, Chief Executive Officer, Streetwise Partners

Congratulations, it's Panel Day. Moderators need to be on top of their game. You should be well-rested, engaged, and ready to embark on a journey of inquiry based on curiosity, a desire to learn, and a desire to share. On the day of the panel, you want to have a plan for the day. It is going to be busy. You are going to be a stage director. You must coordinate with many people to ensure everything goes as planned. Although you may be nervous, you have done lots of preparation, and now you are as ready as you can be for the event.

It's going to be great, but we have provided several checklists to help you and your panelists get ready for the panel.

BEFORE YOU LEAVE HOME

It is easy to forget to bring something on the day of the panel, so the following checklist should help you check off everything you should consider bringing. For example, some of your panelists might have written books you have read, and if you have a copy handy, it is often good to bring it with you, particularly if you plan to refer to a section of it. The following checklist contains

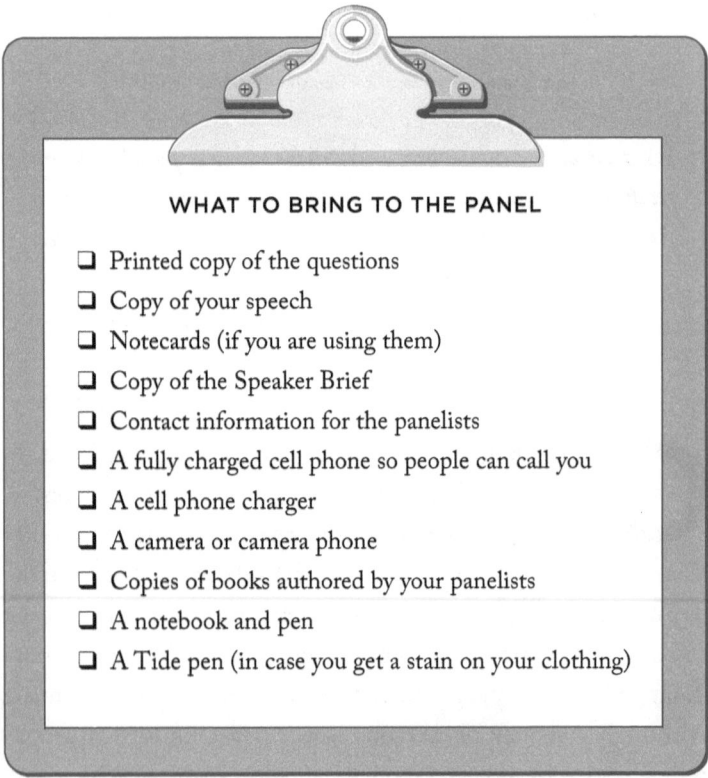

WHAT TO BRING TO THE PANEL

- ❏ Printed copy of the questions
- ❏ Copy of your speech
- ❏ Notecards (if you are using them)
- ❏ Copy of the Speaker Brief
- ❏ Contact information for the panelists
- ❏ A fully charged cell phone so people can call you
- ❏ A cell phone charger
- ❏ A camera or camera phone
- ❏ Copies of books authored by your panelists
- ❏ A notebook and pen
- ❏ A Tide pen (in case you get a stain on your clothing)

a suggested list of items, but if there is something on it you don't feel is necessary, don't bring it. You don't need to bring everything on a camping list to a camping trip; similarly, you don't need to bring everything on this list to your panel.

WHAT TO WEAR

Deciding what to wear to a panel is essential. The event is not a fashion show, but there are factors to consider when moderating a panel that might guide your dress decisions on the day of the event. Dress in a manner that fits your style. If you are comfortable and feel good in what you are wearing, you will be relaxed as you step into your role as a moderator.

Consider how formal the event is. Who will be in the audience, and what would they expect you to wear? Dress up rather than down; I aim to dress one "level" more formal than the audience. For women, I do not recommend wearing short skirts if you are seated on a stage. They can be difficult. If you know the color of your background for the panel, avoid wearing that color or you will blend in. Wearing prints is an easy way to avoid this problem.

The types of technologies being used can also influence your choice of outfit. If you are using a lapel microphone, you will need something to clip it onto, either the collar of a shirt or the lapel of a jacket. If I know I will have an earpiece microphone or a lapel microphone with a belt pack, my preference is to wear a jacket so you can't see the belt pack. Others are happy to clip it to their back, and some people will hold it. Just be aware that dresses often don't provide a good place to put these belt packs, and although I have seen journalists use fancy gadgets to attach the belt pack to their legs, those types of gadgets might not be an option for you.

WHAT TO DO WHEN YOU ARRIVE

Arriving at a conference can be overwhelming. Often, there will be conference organizers who can assist you with this part of the preparation, but in any event, a good moderator ensures the following:

1. When you enter the venue, speak with the person handing out name tags to ensure there are name tags for each panelist. It is best to tell them who you are (the moderator) and instruct them to tell any panelists who arrive where they can find you.
2. Speak with the technical staff and ensure they have enough microphones for each speaker and that the microphones are identical. You should also discuss with the organizers whether they will have staff members roaming through the audience handing microphones to the speakers or whether there will be a microphone on a stand in the aisle that audience members will be asked to line up behind to ask their question.
3. Check the stage one last time. If you plan to have opening remarks given at a podium, make sure the podium is in place. Also, ensure a seat is ready in the wings (if it isn't already on the stage) for every panelist *and yourself*.
4. Ensure there is water for you and the panelists on the podium. Your panelists will be talking for a while, and a dry throat could put them and the entire panel off their game.

BE CORDIAL TO EVERYONE

Be courteous to the support and technical staff. They might be asking you lots of questions, but they are the ones who make the panel happen. Remember that the technical staff, the greeters, the people putting on your microphone, and anyone else you come into contact with, either in the lead up to the panel or on the day of the panel, are there to help you.

Frequently, I tell junior analysts to always be nice to administrators. It isn't just the right thing to do; often, these people come to your rescue when something goes wrong. If you leave your notes on the seat before you come to the podium, the person who greeted you and helped walk you to the stage may be able to help. With technical issues, it's amazing how fast someone can run to the front of the stage with a replacement microphone when they think you are a good person—and how slowly they can make the journey when you've been a jerk to them before the panel.

APPOINT A DESIGNATED PHOTOGRAPHER

Photos don't happen without a photographer. Appoint a friend, work colleague, or one of the conference organizers to take pictures. Make sure you have everyone's permission to use their image if you plan to post photos of the panel on your LinkedIn page. If your panelists don't agree, get your photographer to photograph just you either introducing the panel at the podium or as you moderate. You can also take a photo before the event next to a sign advertising your panel or something that indicates where you are.

Many events have an official photographer and their own official speaker and photography release forms. However, as a moderator, you often don't get access to the pictures. In most cases, the organizers and sponsors of the conference will post the photos in their feeds, and you can link to or comment on their posts. Also, these photos often take time to be released, so having a photo of your own makes it easier and faster for you to create your own post.

MINGLE WITH THE AUDIENCE AND PANELISTS BEFORE THE PANEL

Mingling with the audience is a brilliant insight someone once gave me. If you have the time to speak with one or two audience members before the event, you can ask them why they are there, what they hope to learn from the panel, and what interests them. You can also ask them if they are comfortable with you sharing some of those insights with the audience. Most people are okay with it. As a moderator, you can weave those insights into the panel conversation, making it a richer and more relevant discussion. One moderator I know deals with prepanel nerves by arriving early so they can get a sense of the audience and what they are looking to learn from the panel.

One moderator, Alix Steel, a television anchor for Bloomberg LLP, said that before every panel, she speaks to the panelists and asks them questions about everything but the panel topic: "It's a successful trick because it makes people engaged and invested in the panel. You care about more than just them as experts."

START ON TIME

I cannot emphasize enough the importance of starting on time. This may not be within your control if the prior panel or speaker runs over the allotted time. However, if the panel starts at 9 A.M., start at 9 A.M. I have a spin cycle instructor who tells us when she is late for class that she doesn't like to rush. That is fine, but it is no excuse for starting late. If you don't want to rush, get there early. It's that simple. For those who don't think it is a problem being late, take the perspective of those who showed up at 9 A.M. and are sitting around while you take your time getting on stage.

You might excuse yourself and rationalize that you only started five minutes late, but I ask you what gave you the right to waste the audience's time by doing that.

PREPARE YOURSELF TO GO ON STAGE

Going on stage and speaking in front of a group can be daunting. You're not alone if you experience stage fright to various degrees. Before stepping on stage, take some time to breathe. Giving yourself a quiet five minutes beforehand often helps in quelling nerves. And if you are relaxed at the start of your panel, your panelists will likely be relaxed as well. They will often take their cues from you.

Bring your list of questions. Although I prefer "old-fashioned" hard copies, a digital device can be used. However, I caution that I have seen many moderators trip up on stage because something went wrong with their devices—they have to enter passwords to get the next question, they run out of battery, etc. Even if you plan to use a digital device, bring a paper copy just in case.

Every moderator needs a timer. The smartphone stopwatch function can be used; just press start when the panelist starts answering a question. This is an easy way to time their answer length and an excellent way of ensuring each of your panelists stays on time. You will also want to know when there are five minutes left in the panel; you can either use a digital countdown clock or have someone designated as the timekeeper. Some venues will have a time clock, but do not rely solely on that clock. It might stop or give you insufficient time (particularly if another panel runs over), or your view of the clock might be blocked.

HANDLING NERVES: ADVICE FROM THE EXPERTS

We solicited advice from experts on how they handle prepanel nerves. Here are some of the tips and strategies they found to be successful:

> [I] practice that first couple of sentences and how I'm going to close it out and I practice the transitions.
> —ROBERT S. KRICHEFF, GLOBAL STRATEGIST AND HEAD OF MULTI-ASSET CREDIT, SHENKMAN CAPITAL MANAGEMENT

> [I] always try to get to the location early, so I'm not panicking.
> —JOANNA HOROWITZ, CFA, SENIOR CONSULTANT—ALTERNATIVE INVESTMENT ADVISORY AND CORPORATE RESPONSIBILITY AND DIVERSITY LEAD, BIP. MONTICELLO

> Use mental mantras to psych yourself up for the panel.
> —LISA KAPLOWITZ, ASSOCIATE PROFESSOR, RUTGERS BUSINESS SCHOOL AND EXECUTIVE DIRECTOR OF THE RUTGERS CENTER FOR WOMEN IN BUSINESS (CWIB)

> Keep them chatting right into the panel, and that just kind of takes away all the nerves.
> —ALIX STEEL, TELEVISION ANCHOR, BLOOMBERG LLP

> Icebreakers . . . sometimes they work and sometimes they don't, but depending on the audience, you should consider them.
> —JOYCE CHANG, MANAGING DIRECTOR AND CHAIR, GLOBAL RESEARCH JPMORGAN

Enjoy yourself. At this point, there is little else you can do. You've prepared the panelists and yourself as a moderator, and yes, you might run into some issues, but the main thing to remember is to have fun. That will shine through clearly.

PANELIST PRESTAGE

- ❏ Tell the panelists the order in which they sit
- ❏ Review the ground rules
- ❏ Remind them to smile—everyone loves a friendly face
- ❏ Have them turn off their cell phones or, better yet, leave them with someone in the audience
- ❏ Make sure to remind them to talk directly into the microphone when answering their questions
- ❏ Show them where the time clock is
- ❏ Tell them the expected time that you have allotted for each question answer
- ❏ Review the purpose of the panel
- ❏ Remind them where to look
- ❏ Remind them to speak slowly
- ❏ Remind them to go to the bathroom before the panel starts

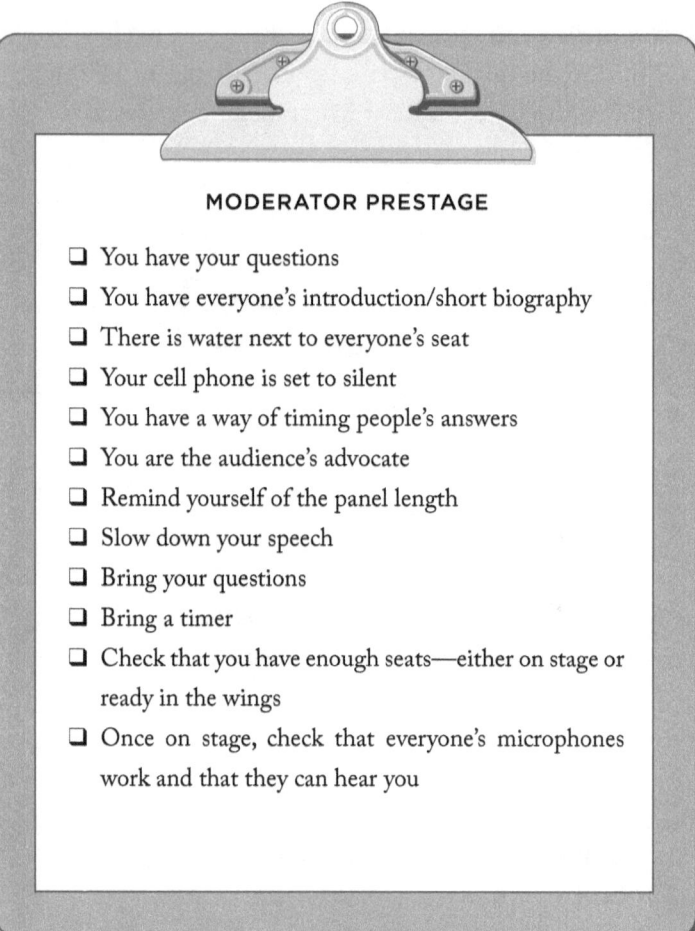

MODERATOR PRESTAGE

- ❏ You have your questions
- ❏ You have everyone's introduction/short biography
- ❏ There is water next to everyone's seat
- ❏ Your cell phone is set to silent
- ❏ You have a way of timing people's answers
- ❏ You are the audience's advocate
- ❏ Remind yourself of the panel length
- ❏ Slow down your speech
- ❏ Bring your questions
- ❏ Bring a timer
- ❏ Check that you have enough seats—either on stage or ready in the wings
- ❏ Once on stage, check that everyone's microphones work and that they can hear you

16

ONSTAGE ADVICE

You are going to make mistakes. You apologize, you don't dwell on it, and you move on.
—Lisa Kaplowitz, Associate Professor, Rutgers Business School and Executive Director of the Rutgers Center for Women in Business (CWIB)

Don't be afraid to be yourself and let your personality shine through.
—Experienced moderator

Be willing to go off script and follow the interesting topics.
—Erin Lyons, Co-Head of CreditSights

MOVING THE PANEL FORWARD

If things go static on the panel, the panel dies. As the moderator, you are in the driver's seat. Just as a driver needs to be in control of the car, a moderator needs to be in control of the panel. Similarly, just as a driver can step on the accelerator to move the car forward, a moderator needs to move a panel forward. The panel cannot be static. You must also ensure the panel does not get "stuck" on one topic.

You can move the panel forward by asking a question that addresses a new aspect of the panel's main discussion topic. If you do this and the panelist continues to refer back to the old topic, you must interrupt them and steer them in the right direction. For example, "Jess, we've spent a lot of time discussing how drug A can help cure this disease. We were hoping to talk about alternative therapies that can supplement it."

In a good panel, where there is much to discuss, keeping the conversation going is easy. Remember that *Top Chef* example from earlier—you opened the basket and found the filet mignon and red wine—you're set. But what if you have more of a mixed basket of panelists? For example, if you have five panelists, you might have one question you are looking for two panelists to opine on. What happens if one of the other panelists also wants to add their opinion? It might be best to allow it, but when a fourth panelist tries to add their opinion, you might have to call it a day on the question.

Panel moderators keep things moving. Although a particular topic might interest the panelists, it might not resonate with your audience members, and spending too much time on it will shorten the amount of time you can spend on other topics that might be of equal or even more interest to the audience. A good moderator is always trying to read the audience and adapt. If a question gets asked during the Q&A session, use it to bring in the fourth and fifth panelists to the conversation if they have indicated they had something to say on the topic. You can also note to yourself that this is a question you can go back to if you have some time at the end of your prepared session. Just don't let the panel get stuck. Keep it moving along.

> Interrupting I think is hard for a panel moderator, because you want the panelists to speak, so a moderator should be willing to

interrupt someone to direct the conversation in a way that keeps moving the conversation forward.

—STEPHEN GROVE, VICE PRESIDENT, GLOBAL DIVERSITY AND INCLUSION, BLACKSTONE

TRANSITIONS

One thing I was worried about was transitioning from one question, to another question, to a different panelist.
—Sarah Auerbach, Managing Director, UniFi by CAIA

Moderators are often given gifts in the answers of panelists. A panelist could make a specific point that summarizes their view exceptionally well. Or they might provide an alarming statistic you want the audience to remember. Pick up on the point and reiterate it. For example, once your panelist Sue has finished answering a question about the importance of libraries in local communities as they democratize access to books, you could say something such as, "Growing up reading library books, I never considered the diversity of the people who were also there borrowing books as well. Thank you, Sue, for reminding us of the importance of libraries in local communities."

Your question list should include some transitions that can help you go from panelist to panelist. Use those, as well as the answers of the panelists, to move the panel along.

BE SPONTANEOUS

One of the best pieces of advice I received just before going on stage was to embrace spontaneity. I'd been preparing for weeks for the panel, had done all the prep calls, rehearsed, and had my list of questions ready. A great moderator is prepared, but to make the audience feel as though the panel is a little more spontaneous and less robotic, they will vary their delivery, use more natural language than formal language, and embrace imperfections. All of this creates the illusion of spontaneity even when the moderator is prepared.

HANDLING LONG-WINDED PANELISTS

Some people don't realize how long they have been talking. Even if you have given your panelists suggested answer lengths, you may still find that one of them goes over—way over—the allotted time. The panelist may just be a talkative person, or you may have touched on a particularly passionate topic and the panelist finds it difficult to control their passion.

How do you know if a panelist is talking too long? First, look at the time clock and see how long they have spoken. If they are well over the allotted time per answer, then it is time to cut them off. Second, trust your judgment. It's probably right. If you feel they have been speaking for too long, they probably have been. Finally, take your cues from the audience.

Feel free to interrupt the panelist. Sometimes, you need to be a little pushy with the panelists, and a good moderator knows when to use their position to cut someone off, redirect the conversation, and move it forward again. As a moderator, cutting off a long-winded panelist will likely be one of the hardest things you need to do, and you must find a way to do it tactfully without offending them.

The more stature the panelist has, the more difficult interrupting them will be. But keep this in the back of your mind. It is your primary mission and purpose as a moderator to ensure your audience has a great experience, and cutting off a long-winded panelist contributes to this. It ensures the audience gets to hear from *all* of the panelists and gets diverse views. It also ensures you don't lose your audience, particularly those who might not be as passionate or as interested in the topic of the monologue.

Don't wait for the panelist to pause before interrupting. It would be easy for a moderator to let these panelists finish or wait for them to breathe before interrupting, but experience has taught me that some panelists have very strong breath control and can talk without pausing. You will need to make a firm but polite interruption to ensure all panelists get equal airtime and you move the panel along. Here are some suggestions:

1. "Derek, let me interrupt you there because I think one of my questions for Jane will touch on some of these points and highlight her experience with diabetes." (Then launch into your question for Jane.)
2. "Allison, I want to jump in here with you. I will remind the audience members that if they want to hear more about the topic, they can find Allison after this panel has ended, and I'm sure she will be able to elaborate further."
3. "Joe, that is an important point you make there. I would love to hear how Cathy responds to your point. Cathy, what are your thoughts?"

Nonverbal cues can also be effective. Capture the panelist's attention with a hand gesture to indicate they need to wrap it up. Or see if you can make eye contact to grab their attention. You could also take a loud, deep breath to indicate to the panelist that it is time for them to finish their point or you will interrupt them soon.

Are you still feeling bad about cutting off someone's bloviation? Just remember the event organizers are on your side. They would have given the panelist the keynote address if they had wanted to hear only from that one panelist.

THE REITERATING PANELIST

Nobody wants to hear someone repeat what someone else has just said. It can be challenging to address this on stage, but if you don't, the discussion may stall if all your panelists do is agree or reiterate. Good, thoughtful preparation can help with this. If you feel someone on the panel has opinions that are similar to those of someone else, physically separate them and make it obvious you want them to focus on their areas of difference.

This is another time when interrupting can be helpful. Think back through your prep call and see if there is something you can use to bring an original thought from the panelist into the conversation. For example, you could say, "Jenny, during our prep call, you shared with me an interesting story about when you handled a similar situation. Could you share that with the audience today?"

HUMOR—SOMETIMES IT ISN'T SO FUNNY

Be careful with humor if it puts down or discounts a group of people. I have listened to comics who make fun of their religion, and although it can be funny, I liken it to walking a tightrope. What might seem humorous to some audience members risks offending many others, so I recommend avoiding humor altogether.

KEEPING TIME

Keep on time. You are the time cop in ensuring each panelist gets fair airtime, but you also need to ensure that when the countdown clock reaches zero, you have finished. If the panel is part of a larger event, you risk taking time from the next speaker. Tactfully end the panel on time. If the panelists have agreed to remain after the panel, let the audience know they will be available to answer questions afterward.

ENDING EARLY

Ending early isn't as bad as you think. If you've gone through all of your questions, including your backup questions, and the audience does not have further questions, consider ending early. Maybe your panel is the event's last panel, and the panel is all that is standing between the audience and networking (or cocktail hour). In this situation, be respectful. End the panel by asking the panelists to sum up the one key message they hope the audience takes from the panel and then conclude the panel. It is not a failure to end early. It just means you allotted too much time for your panel. It happens. However, discussing this with the conference organizers is a good idea. Nobody will complain if the panel ends a few minutes ahead of time, but make sure it ends on a solid note rather than merely fading away.

OH NO, I'M OUT OF QUESTIONS

Sometimes, you might not have the luxury of finishing the panel early, particularly if it is a virtual panel and there is someone scheduled after your panel ends. So what do you do if you run out of questions? Consider coming up with another question for the panelists based on their answers. However, you don't want the question to surprise the panelists. For example, if a few of the panelists mentioned the importance of reading, then ask all the panelists about their favorite book, the book they are currently reading, or what is on their current reading list. Almost every successful person I have met reads extensively.

I have effectively introduced a new question to the panel by providing my answer first and giving the panelists time to develop their own answer. For example, I will say, "I'm about to ask a question about your favorite vacation spot. My favorite vacation spot is the Gold Coast of Australia. Not only does it have some of the best surfing beaches in the world, it has great weather, lots of great seafood, and, most importantly, my family lives there so I get to visit them and take a vacation at the same time. Robert, could you share your favorite vacation spot with the audience?"

ASKING FOR AUDIENCE QUESTIONS

Constantly remind your audience that you will be taking audience questions. Tell them when they will be able to ask their questions and what format you will be using (e.g., note cards, roving microphone, microphone stand at the back, emailed in). If you ask for audience questions and get none (assuming you don't have a planted question), then return to the panelists and continue asking your questions. My favorite line is this: "I have plenty more questions that I would like to ask our panelists, but I want to give our audience the opportunity to jump in as well. So, I'll open the floor to audience questions, and if we don't have any quite yet, then I'll continue with mine."

If you do this, don't forget to survey the audience again after you have asked more questions. Sometimes, it takes some time for the audience to warm up or think of a question, but after a pause, they think of some. You don't want to make one final "ask" for questions, assuming there won't be any once again, and have ten hands go up with only enough time to answer one of the questions.

LETTING YOUR WINNERS RUN

One moderator, Robert S. Kricheff (Global Strategist and Head of Multi-Asset Credit, Shenkman Capital Management), shared one of his favorite panel experiences. Despite being prepared with a list of questions, the panelists took over and had a fantastic debate. As a moderator, you can try and step in (and in this case, Robert did a few times to ensure everyone had a chance to speak), but in this situation, letting the panelists run with it was the most successful strategy:

> I remember the best panel, and I'm probably dating myself. It was between the guy running Cablevision, and the other guy was a broadcaster who was trying to survive, and the final guy had one of the biggest satellite TV franchises at the time. I asked the first question about what the best delivery system was, and they started disagreeing about it. And then one panelist reached down into his tote bag and pulled out a small satellite dish, like the one that goes on the top of your house and said this is what is going to wipe out cable. And word got out at the conference, and the room started filling up because people were saying, you've got to see this. I didn't do anything except make sure the broadband guy got a few words in. It was a great panel because it was fun.

CLOSING OUT THE PANEL

Don't forget to wrap things up and to allow sufficient time for closing out the panel. Consider the following scenario. You are in the midst of an engaging panel conversation, and suddenly, you look down at the time, and it is flashing red. You're about to run out of time. Many moderators make this error, leaving the audience somewhat hanging after having provided them with a wealth of information and having no time to summarize key points from the panel in their conclusion.

There are various ways to close out a panel. Some people like to ask the panelists to provide one key takeaway from panel, which can be effective and a good way of summarizing key messages. Be careful not to ask an open-ended question, such as "Any final thoughts?" You risk having someone go off topic and also risk having your audience disengage because if this is the last question before audience Q&A they are probably getting their questions ready in their heads. Open-ended questions can invite open-ended and very long answers.

A good way to end a panel is to summarize what you have learned. Summarizing the panel discussion helps wrap things up in the minds of the audience. You can do this in multiple ways. One could be asking the panelists, "What's the most surprising thing you've learned during today's discussion?" Another way is to ask your panelists for their closing thoughts on the topics. Although some people find this to be cliché, it is also an excellent way to have your panelists help you close out the panel. Another way is for you to take a key point from one of the answers each panelist has given and use it as your summary. Here is a panel summary I have used in the past.

Audience members, unfortunately, our time together has ended, and what a lot we have all learned today. From Jenny, we learned we should be buying all the homebuilding companies, but from Peter, we were told to stay away from mortgage debt from an investment perspective. Finally, we stepped out of the construction arena. We learned from Sally about opportunities in the cable sector and from Jonathan about new disruptive technologies we need to consider when assessing the long-term prospects of many of our investments. I want to thank our panelists for an engaging panel, and in a few moments, we will have our Fixed Income Investment Opportunities panel.

You might need to close out the panel quickly, particularly if you are running short on time, and you will need to give your panelists an indicator that time is short. In this case, you could say something such as, "Since we are running out of time, in thirty seconds, could you please tell us one hobby you have outside of work?"

17

HANDLING AUDIENCE QUESTIONS

The best part of a panel is when you get the audience to interact, so it isn't question, answer, question, answer where the audience is separate from the panel.
—Alix Steel, Television Anchor, Bloomberg LLP

Audience questions engage the audience in the discussion. Because panels are in service of the needs of the audience, most panels have audience question-and-answer sessions (Q&A). Deciding whether you will have an audience Q&A is a decision to make before the panel. The panelists must agree to receive audience questions, but how you handle them differs depending on the audience. The advantage to you as a moderator is that the audience is doing some of your work for you. They are developing and asking questions. An audience member who asks a question of one or all of the panelists is likely to become more engaged in the panel. They are also more likely to remember the panel, and as we discussed earlier, the purpose of the panel is not only to share an idea or topic with your audience but also to have them share the topic and what they learned from the panel with others.

Open microphones have advantages and disadvantages. As the name suggests, audience members are given the microphone (usually by an usher who roams the audience) and ask questions directly to the panelists. The risk in open-microphone Q&A sessions is that nobody wants to go first. A good moderator often has a "plant" in the audience willing to break the ice and ask the first question. Sometimes, people will place microphones on stands and then have people line up behind them to give answers. I don't recommend this approach. First, you will have a line of people that can be distracting for audience members. Second, you potentially lose some of the "reactive" follow-up questions—audience members who want to follow up on a particular answer will need to "stand in line" to ask.

Smaller rooms might not need audience microphones. However, to ensure that everyone hears the question, you should repeat it if it was asked without a microphone. The person asking the question will be facing forward, so their voice will be directed toward you and the panel. Anyone sitting in the same row or a row further back from them will find it difficult or impossible to hear the question. By repeating the question, you ensure everyone in the room has heard the question.

There are three options for how to choose someone to ask the next question:

1. *Moderator chooses*: Having the moderator choose provides an opportunity to hear from a diverse range of people.
2. *Panelists choose*: I have been at panels where the panelists choose the next person to ask a question, with the moderator working down the line of panelists.
3. *Person walking around with the microphone chooses*: This can work, but you risk having less question diversity or potentially having all your questions come from one section of the room.

I do not recommend having a microphone passed from questioner to questioner. It risks only being available to a small group of potentially "related" people in the audience. If you can't easily see the audience and have no one who can act as a roaming microphone holder, then despite its disadvantages, use a microphone stand.

OTHER WAYS OF RECEIVING QUESTIONS

1. *Notecards*: Place notecards on each seat before the panel, so audience members can write their questions down and hand them to the ushers during the panel. The benefit of this is that audience members will write the questions when they are fresh in their minds.

    Having audience members write their questions on cards can be a great idea for a variety of reasons. Not everyone enjoys asking questions in public, so having them write down their questions will allow more people to ask questions. It will also help you ensure the quality of questions is good. You might get two cards with similar questions you can combine into one. Having questions asked on cards makes it easy for people to ask anonymous questions. As a moderator, you can eliminate the risk of an inappropriate question because you can cut those cards up front. Finally, questions on cards eliminate people who make comments rather than ask questions. That said, the challenge is sorting the questions in real time. I handle this by creating a mini filing system on stage using my fingers as the dividers. I place similar questions together in groups separated by my fingers and then create a stack by placing the piles in alternate directions.

2. *Digital Question Submission*: Many conferences now have a digital app that allows attendees to submit questions before

or during the panel. These questions can be distributed to the moderator on a television screen during the Q&A portion of the panel. In virtual panels there are many Q&A features that you can use to receive questions from the audience.

3. *Prepanel Questions*: If you request questions before the panel, you have the most control over audience questions. If you use this method, you must include the question request in the invitation sent to audience members and the reminder emails sent closer to the event. As a moderator, you can choose which questions make the most sense, depending on the questions you plan to ask, your backup questions, and what you believe will be of most interest to the audience.

AUDIENCE POLLING

New technologies have made polling easy. To see if the panel has influenced or changed their view on a particular topic, you can take audience polls before and after your panel. This is a great way to gauge the event's effectiveness and provide information you can give back to the panelists. It also provides good data the media can use.

Conducting a warmup poll is easy, and there are many different polling tools you can use. The benefit of prepanel polling is that you involve your audience in the discussion ahead of the panel. You can publish the results on the screen and get your panelists to comment or ask them whether they are surprised at some of the answers.

Polling doesn't have to be formal. It can be as simple as "Raise your hand if . . ." A fun way of engaging an audience is to start with a question most people will answer "yes" to (and raise their hand). You can then follow that question up with "Now keep your hand raised if . . ." and, if it makes sense, follow it up with a question such as "Now leave your hand still raised if . . ."

Another form of polling that is easy to implement in a digital world is a word poll, where panelists type a word into the poll and those words are aggregated and displayed on the screen in real time. You can use the words to create a word cloud. You can ask questions such as "What is your favorite food?" or "What do you think of when you think of investing?" The options are endless. Figure 17.1 shows a word cloud of preferred movie and television genres. The downside of a digital poll is that when the audience pulls out their cell phone to answer the polling question, they might get distracted by text messages or work email.

For an educational panel, a warmup poll can be a helpful way of gauging the audience's knowledge. "How many of you have a financial advisor?" could be a polling question. Or you could ask a question such as, "Do you intend to pursue a career in architecture?" before a career panel, with "definitely yes," "almost definitely yes," "maybe," "no," and "unsure" as your answer options. If you have designed your panel to debunk a myth or multiple myths about a profession, you can take a similar poll after the panel to assess the impact.

FIGURE 17.1 Preferred movie and television genres.

Prepanel polling has advantages. Doing it before the event means you don't lose panel discussion time as audience members log into the polling website and register their answers. The downsides are that only some people respond to prepanel polling and you will also lose some of the excitement and energy polling creates. An excellent solution to the latter problem is to include an audience poll during the panel but complement it with a prepanel poll.

QUESTIONS IN THE MIDDLE OR AT THE END OF A PANEL

A moderator controls the event flow. This includes deciding when to open the panelists to audience questions during the panel. Although we don't want to insult our audience members, they often ask questions that don't flow well together. The questions can be very narrow or specific. As a result, I find it is best to leave audience questions until the end of the panel particularly for panels under one hour in length.

Regardless of when you take questions, you want to ensure the audience is ready with their questions when you launch into the Q&A, so you should frequently remind your audience to get their questions ready. When the clock indicates that there are only a few minutes until you begin taking audience questions, you should remind the audience that the Q&A will be starting soon. This reminder will also signal to the tech team that questions are forthcoming, especially if there are roving microphones.

PLANTED AUDIENCE QUESTIONS

The worst thing that can happen during audience Q&A is silence. Sometimes, nobody wants to be the first person to ask a question. A way to avoid this is to "plant" a question with a friendly audience member. Ask someone comfortable with public speaking to ask the first question. They can ask a question you have given to them or a question of their own. It does not matter.

The other time a planted question can be helpful is at the end of the audience Q&A. If you are trying to keep the panel on time (which is part of your role as the moderator), having your last question come from someone who wants to deliver a diatribe before asking their question can result in the panel running over the allotted time. You also want to end on a high note, not a sour note, so having an uplifting final question helps.

Please don't fear that you are manipulating your audience by doing this. If you use a plant for the first question, you may find yourself with a very excited person who raises their hand quickly once the first question has been asked. Ask them to ask their question rather than going to the person with the planted question. As we have said repeatedly throughout this book, a great panel is all about preparation, which includes preparing for when things don't go as expected. Not having a first question is one of those situations, so having a plant is a great way to prevent this situation from disrupting your panel's flow.

QUESTIONER DIVERSITY

As a moderator, you want diversity in the people asking questions. As you select who to call on when you have a roving microphone, please ensure you choose a diverse group of people. Although you will have to make some assumptions based on appearance, the benefits of doing this will more than offset the costs of making the initial judgment, which only needs to exist for the duration of the question period. Call on people both young and old, men and women, eager individuals who raise their hand fast and enthusiastically, and those who are timid and raise their hand less quickly and less high. Your audience will benefit from having such a diverse range of perspectives in the room. Too often, women do not raise their hands. Deliberately ensure that you are encouraging women as well as men to ask questions.

LIGHTNING ROUND

A lightning round features questions with fast, lightning-speed answers. It is a format I have found to be successful, particularly in large audiences. I have audience members submit questions to an email address or website and use them to create a lightning round of questions. Usually, the lighting round happens toward the end of the panel. During the lightning round, I ask one of the panelists (and one only) to answer a question I received and then give them sixty seconds to respond. I use a buzzer to let the panelist know when they reach sixty seconds to keep the questions moving fast.

Other panelists often ask to jump in after the first panelist has answered. I allow this but keep their follow-up thoughts within the same sixty-second time limit. Adding lots of fast questions makes a panel fun and engaging for the audience. They get a quick answer to the question and often an alternative perspective, and if your panelists have agreed to stay around after the event, the person asking the question can approach the panelist directly to get more information and to follow up.

THE WORST QUESTIONS

The worst questions start with something like, "This is more of a comment than a question." It is as though the person is disappointed they aren't on the panel and are using audience Q&A to share their expertise. If it is a quick comment, let it go, but if it runs longer, you can interrupt the audience member in the same way as described previously for a long-winded panelist. One option is to say, "We have a limited amount of time and a lot of hands. Can you reframe your comment as a brief question for the panelist, or can we move on to one of our other audience members?"

You can also turn a comment into a question. For example, if someone says, "Based on my experience, I believe it is important for all teachers to have a master's degree in education because if they don't, we won't be providing the best education to our children," you can turn the comment into a question based on your knowledge of the panelists (again, another reason having those individual panelist calls can be helpful) and say something like, "Ramona, when you began your teaching career, you didn't have your master's. Do you think you were still qualified to teach then?"

FUN FACTS

Fun questions are a fun way to end a panel. Some suggestions include the following:

"What hobby did you pick up during COVID?"
"What is the signature dish you cook?"
"If you weren't in this job, what would you do?"
"For vacations, do you prefer to camp in the wild, hang out in a spa at the Ritz, bungee jump, or go to Disney World?"

18

PANEL HICCUPS

Things will go wrong—it's inevitable. Preparing for a panel means doing everything outlined in this book, from having a Speaker Brief to having everyone's alternative contact information. It also means thinking about all the things that could go wrong and having a strategy for handling them. If you are prepared for these common hiccups, you might find that the only person who knows something went wrong is you.

THE ABSENT PANELIST

A panelist does not turn up—no worries, you've prepared additional questions for the other panelists as part of your panel preparation, so you will use those extra questions to cover for the missing panelist. Sometimes, a panelist runs late. How to handle this situation is up to you and depends on how late the panelist is. If the panelist is a vital part of the discussion, explain what happened to the audience and have the panelist join you as soon as they arrive. In the interim, hold their questions until they are seated and then give them time to breathe before jumping in. Also, when setting up a question, you might want to say something like, "Panelist Y believes in the power of positive body images. Your research suggests a more nuanced interpretation. Can you help the audience understand?" This helps get the late panelist up to speed (telling them what the other panelist said) and gives them a chance to respond.

TECHNICAL DIFFICULTIES

I have never met a moderator who hasn't encountered technical difficulties, so you should prepare. We have discussed strategies to help you familiarize yourself with technology. This minimizes the likelihood of technical difficulties. But things happen, so you must prepare for and be able to address any issues. For example, at the start of a panel, I got an indicator that the audio on the webcast was not working. We stopped the panel as the tech crew addressed it.

One common technical problem is that the lapel microphones do not work. Don't let this bother you—ask for a roaming microphone and continue the discussion. It may be more cumbersome, but you can continue the conversation. If just one of the lapel microphones isn't working, you must make a game-day decision: Do you ask for a new one or go with the roaming microphone? Check with your panelists and ask them what they would prefer.

Another problem that can occur is that the audio may not work—yes, it happens. In this case, there isn't much you can do. Find out from the tech team how long it will take to fix the issue, and then when you get restarted, ask the team in charge to reset the clock. You might lose some of your panel time to accommodate the technical interruption, but organizers should try and ensure you get as much of your original panel time as possible.

Some technical difficulties can last much longer than expected, and as the moderator, you will have to decide what to do. If the audio isn't reaching your webcast audience but you have live audience members in the room, give it a few minutes and then continue. Ask someone to take notes to share with the webcast audience. Having your live audience wait until the webcast audio is fixed isn't a good use of their time. You could ask the panelists a "filler" question as you wait for the audio to be fixed, such as "Where is the best place you have visited over the last year?" The question should be something the webcast audience will not miss. You will then need to look for the cue that the audio is working before starting the panel. Losing audio seems like it would never happen, but I have experienced it.

To ensure you give the audience as much value as possible when there is a technical problem, think of creative solutions. You could have the panelists provide a written answer to one of the unasked questions and distribute the answers to the audience via email afterward. Be creative. People have turned up for your event and given their time. You want to show that you value their time and are doing everything possible to compensate for the unplanned technical difficulty.

OUTSIDE NOISE

Disruptions occur in many different forms. You are moderating a panel, and next door, someone starts jackhammering. I've only seen it happen to someone else, and I wasn't on the panel involved. When the interruption occurred, someone at the organization worked to stop it as quickly as possible. If there isn't a representative in the room, have someone on your team act quickly to minimize the noise disruption.

Try talking over noise disruption. Acknowledge it is happening and then try to work through it. Another alternative is to ask the panelists a fun question while someone stops the noise interruption.

YOU DIRECT A QUESTION TO THE WRONG PANELIST

I once had a panel with two people who had the same first name. After carefully preparing the questions and ensuring the panelist order rotated, the "wrong" Tom answered the question, and suddenly, I was off my game. What did I do? I didn't stop "wrong" Tom from speaking: it wasn't fair to him, and it was only me who knew he should not have been speaking on this point. I then had the "right" Tom answer it. When it came to evening the score and ensuring that all panelists got equal airtime, I directed the "wrong" Tom to answer one of his questions quickly by beginning my question for him with the phrase, "In just one quick sentence..."

HIDDEN AGENDAS

Some panelists have hidden agendas. As the name suggests, they are invisible, so it is your job as moderator to determine whether any panelists have one. It helps if you are aware of such agendas as you research each panelist and look for them each time you engage with the panelists before the panel, including during the ask, the individual panelist calls, and the prepanel call with all of your panelists. Having a panelist who is heavy-handed with feedback on your questions and tries to add questions that are irrelevant to the panel's mission is a clue they might have a hidden agenda. Forewarned is forearmed.

I HAVE TO TAKE THIS CALL

Ringing cell phones are a feature of most panels today. There are multiple ways to handle them, from reminding people in advance to silence their phones to stopping the conversation and seeing what the call is about. Most people are embarrassed they forgot to turn off their cellphones, so if they take care of it quickly and silence the phone, I don't have a big problem with that.

Sometimes, you will see an audience member pick up their phone and take a call while walking out. Obviously, it would be better if they didn't take the call, but if they have to, then the most appropriate way is to try and wait to exit the room before answering or answer and quickly say, "Please hold on for just a moment." You never know why someone must take a call but assume positive intent. The person was part of the audience and wanted to hear what the panelists had to say. Maybe they have a sick relative, the school is calling, or a young child has reached out.

THE PANELIST INTERRUPTER

Some panelists like to interrupt and start speaking over fellow panelists. If this occurs and the less aggressive panelist cedes the floor, you have two options. You could allow it and then take a question away from the interrupter, or you could show some leadership as moderator and take control of the situation. You might have to say, for example, "Jack, let me pause you there because I think Jill was still completing her answer, and I want to ensure we have her full opinion before moving to your different view of the situation."

It takes nerve, but it is also part of being a leader. A great moderator can take back control of the panel and make sure everyone on the panel gets the opportunity to provide a complete answer to the question.

DISRUPTIVE AUDIENCE MEMBERS

Disrupters often show up in the audience. You know the type. During a panel, they are the type of person who shares their opinion under the guise of asking a question. In a facilitated group, the disrupter causes trouble, making it harder for the group to work together. Dealing with rabble-rousers takes the right balance of poise, diplomacy, and sternness. Give the disruptive audience member a gentle warning, such as, "If we can hold all comments and questions until the formal part of the panel is finished, we will have an audience question-and-answer session at the end." If the disrupter has a political statement they want to make, politely remind them that this isn't the proper forum and allow them to sit down and cease their questionable behavior without losing face. It helps if you are stern. Otherwise, you risk the negative behavior continuing, undermining the entire event.

Someone in the audience might comment on what a panelist is saying, particularly if they disagree. As a moderator, you must work to silence disruptive audience members. You should prepare a list of responses to disrupters before the event rather than trying to think of a response on the day of the event. Some suggestions include the following: "Thank you for sharing your opinion, but we would ask you to hold such comments and questions until the end of the panel when we have allotted time for the panelists to address your questions" and "We remind the audience that interruptions while our panelists are talking are not welcome, and repeated interrupters will be asked to leave."

RESERVED PANELISTS

Quiet panelists can be a challenge for even the most skilled moderator. They often give very short answers, speak quietly, and appear reluctant. It might initially be nerves, and in this case, hopefully, they will warm up with time. But if you have a very reserved panelist, you might need to shift strategies partway through the panel. For example, if Panelist C does not give long answers, you can solicit their opinion after either Panelist A or Panelist B has spoken. Your prep call will be helpful in this situation as well because you will be able to delve into your knowledge bank of information and see if you can ask the reserved panelist a question, such as, "Panelist B has given us an excellent set of reasons why we should have integrated suburbs, which seems very similar to having diversity in our suburbs. You have researched diversity. Would you agree there are benefits to having more diverse suburbs, and what could we do to achieve that?"

GOING OFF TOPIC

During the panel, you may find that one of your panelists diverges from the topic, and you need to know whether to interrupt and redirect them, let them finish and then move on, or cut them off entirely. As a moderator, you must always be aware of the panel's purpose and ensure that the panelist's answer stays on topic as much as possible.

SHORT ANSWERS

If you have a panelist who gives answers that are too short, you should ask a follow-up question. You can ask one of your backup questions or have the panelist elaborate on something they said in their original answer.

For example, when talking about mentorship, one panelist mentioned she had worked at three different firms during her career. When her answer ended sooner than the allotted time, the follow-up question I asked was, "As a senior female leader, what obstacles did you have to overcome when you changed firms?" It wasn't a surprise question because we had discussed it previously, and it allowed her to extend her answer time.

A DISENGAGED AUDIENCE

A disengaged audience is easy to identify once you see it but difficult to define. Your panelists could give dull answers, causing you to lose your audience. In situations like this, moderator presence and leadership come into play. It is your job to inject some life into the panel discussion, making the panel more engaging and creating energy for the audience.

Recognizing the signs that you have lost your audience is hard but necessary. You will start to hear paper rustling or start to feel movement in the room or a lot of coughing. People begin shifting around in their seats, itching to get up and leave. They might be bored by the panel or by one of the speakers, or it could be the end of the day and they are tired.

It is your job as a moderator to reengage the audience. Here are some methods for reengaging your audience:

1. Poll the audience with a raising of their hands.
2. Have the audience all stand up, move around in their spot for a minute, and then sit down again. This strategy is particularly effective if they have been sitting for over an hour.
3. Shorten the allotted answer time and use some of your additional questions to increase the pace of the event.

You are there to engage the audience. If a panelist is speaking and you can clearly see the audience is bored, interrupt the panelist. It doesn't matter if they are sharing the cure for cancer: no one is listening, and you know the saying, "If a tree falls in the forest and nobody hears it, does it make a sound?" If no one hears the message, then the message has no impact.

AUDIENCE QUESTION ISSUES

Sometimes audience questions are directed at one panelist only. This is a difficult situation, particularly when you have a superstar panelist and everyone wants to ask them a question. In this situation, you can include the other panelists in the discussion by taking a phrase out of the superstar's answer and using it to pose a question to another panelist.

However, you must also remember that these are the audience's questions, not yours, and if they are particularly interested in hearing the views of one panelist, you should meet their needs. Hopefully, you can include the other panelists in the question-and-answer session, but remember that this part of the panel is all about the audience rather than the panelists. In addition, you should have prepared the panelists in the panel prep call that this might happen. Finally, as stated previously, although you want the time each panelist spends speaking to be fair, it might not necessarily be equal. A situation like this is one such case where it won't be equal.

Sometimes the audience doesn't realize you are a moderator, not a panelist, and will ask you a question directly. The best thing to do is to dismiss it as quickly as possible because the panel isn't about you and you should not be sharing your opinions and thoughts on the topic.

19

AFTER THE EVENT

Pat yourself on the back! You did it. You hosted a successful panel. But your job is not done once you leave the venue.

Being a moderator is a great job. You are the event's ringmaster, which is a vital role. You must deal with the pressure of ensuring things go smoothly, but if the panel runs well and results in a good conversation, you have been a big part of ensuring the panel's success. However, you want the attendees to remember the performance of the panelists rather than your performance as a moderator.

POSTPANEL QUESTION TIME

Your run of show might have included a postpanel question time. This should be limited to a few minutes after the panel as a time when audience members can approach panel members individually. You should be present during this time to be respectful of the panelists' time—you can let everyone know when their time is up.

BUILDING RELATIONSHIPS

Nurture the relations that you build with your panelists. As moderator, you are uniquely positioned to build your knowledge base, showcase it, and expand your professional expertise and network. Make sure your panelists exchange contact information after the panel. Exchanging email addresses will help them develop their network, which is a benefit of being on the panel.

Send individual thank-you emails or notes to each panelist. According to etiquette professionals, an email should be sent within twenty-four hours, but you have a week to send a handwritten note. In the email or note, mention something specific you learned from the panelist.

If the event is being recorded, ask for a link to the recording. You can post the recording link to your social media channel and tag the other panelists. It is good press for you and them. If you have a photo of the event, you can post the photo (either of you individually or the entire panel if you have their permission) and provide a brief description of the event and the key things you learned from the panel discussion. Use engaging words, and rather than start the post with "I just hosted a panel . . ." use engaging statistics to capture your LinkedIn audience's attention. For example, "Did you know that 52 percent of sea turtles will encounter plastic in their lifetime and 22 percent of those sea turtles will die? I just hosted a successful panel of key scientists on the topic of waste in our oceans where I learned about safe ways to clean our oceans and ways to discourage littering that can kill sea animals." You might feel like this is bragging, but it provides publicity for everyone at the event. Consider how it will help build your brand and personal and professional network and could lead to other moderating and career opportunities.

In addition, you are helping your panelists build their networks and brands if you mention their names in your post, which could lead to business opportunities and other speaking engagements. It's a win-win all around.

FEEDBACK FROM YOUR PANELISTS

You should host a postpanel call to get feedback from the panelists on how the panel went, what they found to be successful, and so on. You might not be able to do this as a group call, but you should follow up individually. Feedback is a gift. Your panelists are taking time to give it to you, and you should consider it and use it to improve as a moderator.

POSTPANEL MARKETING

Postpanel marketing differs depending on the panel's purpose. Depending on why the panel was hosted, different types of postpanel marketing and events can help you get the maximum benefit from the panel.

- *Informational panel*: You could conduct an interview with each panelist after the event to record them discussing what they learned from the panel or information they want to share.
- *Fundraising panel*: You could interview each panelist, if appropriate, about why they support the organization. What aspects of the organization's mission appeal to them?
- *Sales panel*: You should get each panelist to record a testimonial for the product that you can use on the product's promotional website.

Be imaginative in leveraging the panel's content. If the media was present at the event, follow up with them to see if they are interested in writing an article about it. I mentioned having a QR code at the panel, and those links can be reused, repackaged, and sent to audience members after the conclusion of the event. The links could be to papers written by the panelists, relevant studies, or helpful resources and websites.

PANEL EVALUATION

Every panel should seek feedback from the audience. If the organizer polled the audience after the panel, ask them to share the results with you. Depending on the sensitivity of the comments, consider sharing the feedback with the panelists. Make the feedback neutral if it isn't or tactfully identify areas of improvement. Audience feedback can help you improve your ability to moderate panels and learn what type of panelists are the most effective with audiences. Some panelists might ask for feedback, either the official feedback or your personal feedback on the panel and how it went. If you can, you should send out a postpanel questionnaire to the audience. Here are some sample questions you could include in the questionnaire:

- Please rate each of the speakers and their knowledge of the topic.
- How accurate was the event description?
- Was the information you learned in the session useful? If yes, in what way? If not, why?
- Was the information you learned from the panel new to you?
- Would you recommend this panel to a friend or colleague?

OVERCOMING BAD MODERATING EXPERIENCES

We've all had bad experiences, and you might moderate a panel that is poorly received. Don't simply blame the panelists for this outcome. Look at ways you can improve your skills as a moderator.

Don't let one bad experience stop you from accepting more moderator opportunities. So a panel session didn't go as planned; that is in the past, and it shouldn't stop you from moving forward and improving. It is said that learning how to fail and learning from those failures make a great athlete, executive, or student. Don't think of yourself as a failed moderator. Think of it as gaining valuable experience and learn from that experience. Despite reading this book, you will likely face hurdles even the best moderators would struggle to handle. As my father always told me, if you fall over, get back up, dust yourself off, and keep going.

We are often our own harshest critics. First, the panel probably wasn't as bad as you perceived it to be—don't forget that, often, only you and the panelists will know you messed up a particular question. Second, we learn from our failures. They make us better and stronger. Think of a "bad" moderator experience as a learning experience. You now know what *not* to do next time, which makes you a much better moderator than before the "disaster."

TELL YOUR BOSS ABOUT IT

At the beginning of the book, we mentioned the career benefits of being a moderator. But if you moderate a successful panel and no one knows, do you get credit for it? Probably not.

Email your boss after the event and let them know what happened. Tell them about the preparation you did, the number of people in the audience, and other details. Share any feedback you received either informally or formally. If you have an internal company website for sharing information, have an article written about the panel and your involvement.

FIND THE NEXT MODERATOR OPPORTUNITY

You're now a pro, and it's time to leverage your experience and find the next moderator opportunity. Tell organizations you belong to that you are open to facilitating and organizing panels. Email their educational coordinator or meeting coordinator with photos and feedback from the panel(s) you have moderated.

Let your friends and colleagues know you are interested in moderating panels because they may hear about opportunities and refer you to the organizer as someone to consider for the panel. Being able to handle "difficult" panelists is considered a prized skill by many panel organizers. You want to make sure you showcase your talent in this area. For example, I became known as a moderator who could adeptly manage a panel of men with large egos. I was often asked to moderate five intelligent, enthusiastic, and passionate hedge fund managers who had a lot of information to share with the audience. How did I measure this success? I got direct feedback from the audience and the event organizers. I also got feedback from the panelists who felt they were given equal time to pitch, had the opportunity to convey their expertise, and had received their fair share of questions. The ability to handle difficult panelists is a rare talent, and making your skills known in this area guarantees many future moderator opportunities.

In the same way you searched for and found your panelists, event hosts will search for and research panel moderators.

They will look at your LinkedIn page and see if you have experience in the field that aligns with the panel topic. They will also want to know where you live to see if it is close to the panel's location. Finally, they will read your biography and LinkedIn profile to try and understand more about your personality, so ensure your profile is engaging and lively.

Some event hosts will want to interview you before asking you to moderate a panel at their event. They will assess the types of questions you ask them about the event, your conversational tone, whether you are engaging in conversation, and whether you have an online presence that matches the brand they support. They want to know whether you will engage with the audience and whether you have the skills to bring the audience into the conversation in a controlled manner.

Finally, a great event coordinator will be listening to hear about how you intend to prepare for the panel and how much

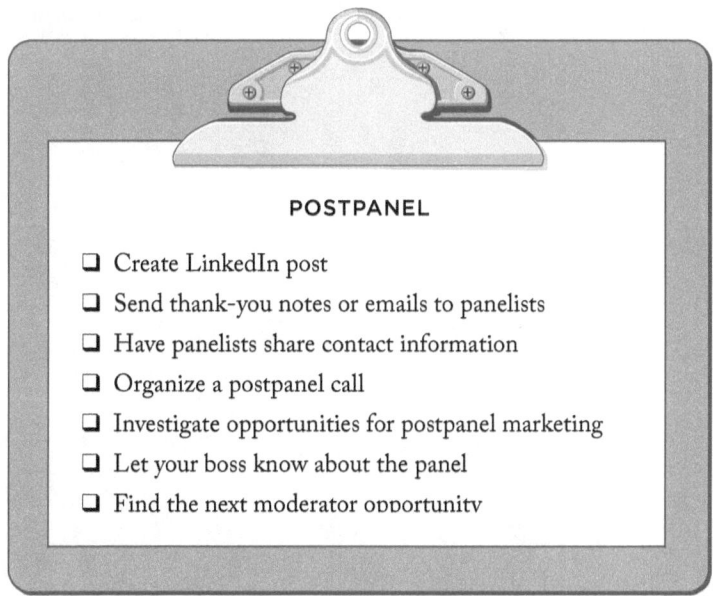

POSTPANEL

- ❏ Create LinkedIn post
- ❏ Send thank-you notes or emails to panelists
- ❏ Have panelists share contact information
- ❏ Organize a postpanel call
- ❏ Investigate opportunities for postpanel marketing
- ❏ Let your boss know about the panel
- ❏ Find the next moderator opportunity

effort you will put into the role. They don't want someone who will take a backseat and watch the panel unfold before them. Instead, they want someone who will take the time to get to know the panelists, do their research on the topic, and prepare to create wonder and curiosity in the audience members.

INDEX

abilities showcased, 39–40
absent panelist, 189–190
academic panel, 70
advertising, 132
advice, for first-time moderators, 146
advice, for organizers: moderator choice relating to, 142; panelists selection, 143–144; panel purpose relating to, 142; on panel time, 144; on panel topic, 144; on technology, 145; on travel reimbursement, 146
advice, for panelists, 131, 141–142; individual prep call relating to, 132–133; panel preparation relating to, 133–134, 137; pointers relating to, 138–140; questions relating to, 134–136
advice, onstage, 175–179; humor with, 174; for long-winded panelists, 172–174; panel moved forward, 169–171; spontaneity with, 171–172; transitions as, 171

Anderson, Chris, 153
anecdotes, 134, 155
anxiety: Carr on, 159; on moderator, 26; on preparation, 104; on questions, 101
the "ask," 177; connection emails, 59; information relating to, 59–60; LinkedIn, 59; media relating to, 59–61; sample emails, 61–62
Aspen Institute, global leadership programs of, vii–viii
"Aspen Socratic Method," vii
assemblage, of panel, 32
audience, 11; data concerning, 48–49; experience of, 47–48; feedback from, 202, 204; goals of, 5; mingling with, 164; read of, 170; technology relating to, 49; understanding of, 47–51, 57
audience polling, 49, 74–76, 98–99, 183–185, 197

audience questions, handling of, 176–177, 184, 187–188, 197–198; digital question submission, 182–183; engagement with, 180; microphones relating to, 181–182; notecards, 182; panelist choice with, 181; "plant" with, 181, 185–186; prepanel, 183
Auerbach, Sarah, 38, 171
awareness raising, 44–45

benefits, to panelists: enhancement, of credibility, 132; expertise highlighted, 131–132; free advertising, 132; of opening speeches and panelist introductions, 117–119. *See also* career benefits
biographies, 86, 130
bloviation, 174
board members, 56
body language, 156–157
Bolton, Deirdre: on audience, 47; on The Holy Grail, 1; on messages, 20; on topic, 51; on visibility, 38
book authors, 57
boredom, panel with, 65–66
boss, of moderator, 203–204
brainstorming, 43, 102
brand, 200–201
Brown, Brene, 155–156
Brown, Sean: on audience, 11; on interruptions, 79; on preparation, 15; on prep session, 88; on technology, 74
buffer time, 32
business cards, 140

camera, 77–78
career benefits, 38–40, 41, 203; abilities showcased, 39–40; executive presence, 39; leadership skills, 39; networking, 38; relationship enhancement, 38, 39; self-assurance, 39; visibility, 38
Carr, Ellen: on anxiety, 159; on moderator, 26; on preparation, 104; on questions, 101
Chang, Joyce, 7, 153, 166
changemaker skills, vii–xix, 2
characteristics: of audience, 48; of moderator, 25–29; of panelists, 140–142
checklist, 10–12, 16, 160–161
close out, of panel, 178–179
colloquy panel, 69–70
commercialism, 137–138
commitment, to moderating, 31–32, 35–37
communication, 29–30, 52; corporate concerns with, 38; policies with, 36; protocol with, 82. *See also* storytelling
comprehensiveness, 13–14
conference website, 128
conflicts, of interest, 34–35
contact information, 200
content, for panel, 97, 99–100, 133–134
continuing education, 45
continuing professional education (CPE) credit feature, 98
contributions, of panelists, 58
corporate communication concerns, 36

courtesy, 162–163
COVID-19, 68, 77
CPE. *See* continuing professional education credit feature
creative marketing ideas: CPE credit feature, 98; marketing, 97–98, 191; panelist featuring, 98; panelist highlighting, 97–98; recorded promotion, 98
credibility, 132
crowdsourcing questions, 111–112
curiosity, of audience, 153–154

data, 48–49, 145–146
debate panel, 69
debates, 18–19, 25
demanding panelists, 64–65
digital question submission, 182–183
direction and flow, of panel, 102–103
diversity: of panelists, 62–63; questioner, 186–187; of views, 173
Dowling, Harlem, 2
drafting, of opening speeches and panelist introductions, 120

education. *See* continuing professional education credit feature
educational panel, 184
emails, 77, 127, 204; connection, 59; follow up, 92–93; sample, 61–62; thank-you, 200
emotions, 156–157
engagement, of audience, 150–151, 154–155, 180, 196–197;
"equal feeling space," 158
executive presence, 39

expectations, 48, 83, 88–89, 143
experience: of audience, 47–48; learning, 38; of moderator, 203; of panelists, 58
expertise, 81, 131–132
extrovert panelist, 81–82

facilitated session participant, 24
facilitators, 23–24
feedback, 79, 123; from audience, 202, 204; after interviews, 22–23; from panelists, 201
filler words, 151–152
Finance Leaders Fellowship (FLF), viii
fireside chat, 54–55
first-time moderator, 146
FLF. *See* Finance Leaders Fellowship
focus, of moderator, 150
focus group, 23
follow up emails, 92–93
format, of panel, 68–71
"friendly" panelist, 55–56
friend raising, 45–46
Fu, Scarlet, 117, 131
fun, with panel, 153–154
fundraising, 45–46, 201
fun facts, 114–115, 188

Gatto, Michael, 53, 131
Gibbs, Anita, 30, 30n5
Gibson, Faith, 29, 29n4
global leadership programs, vii–viii
goals: of audience, 5; of panel, 2–3, 17
"gotcha" questions, 113–114
group, focus, 23

Group Prepanel Prep Call, 92
group prep calls: expectations set during, 88–89; follow-up emails relating to, 92–93; moderator role discussed during, 89–90; panelists title, 89
Grove, Stephen, 4, 43, 171

headshot, 86
Horowitz, Joanna: on learning experience, 38; on time, 166
"How to be a Great Moderator," 12
how-to-guide: comprehensiveness relating to, 13–14; panel relating to, 8–17; preparation relating to, 15–17; templates and checklists for, 10–12, 16
humor, 149, 174

identification, of potential panelists, 57–59; sponsoring organization for, 56
Individual Prepanel Prep Call, 87
individual prepanel prep calls, 124; expectations during, 83; headshot and biography relating to, 86; information flow during, 85; reimbursement information during, 86; research during, 83; strategies during, 84–85
individual prep call, questions during, 132–133
information, 44, 82, 105, 145–146; contact, 200; during prep calls, 85–86; with "the ask," 59–60. *See also* Speaker Brief

informational panel, 201
"information dump," 153
interests: of audience, 48; conflicts of, 34
Internet, 82, 119
interruptions, 79; handling of, 170–174, 193–195
interviews, 104–105; definition of, 21, 21nn2–3; feedback after, 22–23; listening with, 22, 25–26; preparation for, 22; writing for, 22
introductions. *See* opening speeches, panelist introductions and
introvert panelist, 81–82

job, of moderator, 18, 18n1
Jobs, Steve, 154

Kaplowitz, Lisa: on engagement, 28; on mental mantras, 166; on mistakes, 169; on preparation, 104; on prep calls, 88
Kohomban, Jeremy: on energy, 77; on questions, 2; on voice, 147; on worst panel, 81
Kricheff, Robert S., 118, 166, 177; on worst panels, 53, 81
Krohn, Logan, 54, 62
Krull, Shari: on energy, 15; on storytelling, 155

lapel microphones, 190
leadership skills, 39
length, of opening speeches and panelist introductions, 118–119, 120–121

lightning round, 187
LinkedIn, 200, 205; messenger feature in, 59; photos in, 163; profiles in, 57; website for, 130
listeners, 22, 25–26
logistics, 124–125, 128. *See also* structure and logistics
long *vs.* short panel, 76
long-winded panelists, 174; interruptions with, 172–173; nonverbal cues with, 173
Lyons, Erin, 67–68, 169

media. *See* Social Media and Event Promotion Guide
membership building, 45
messenger feature, in LinkedIn, 59
metaphors, 134
microphones, 74–75, 181–182, 190
misalignment, of purpose, 34–35
moderator, 1–2, 26, 146, 203; audience questions relating to, 181, 185; characteristics of, 25–29; choice of, 142; focus of, 150; opportunities for, 204–206; presence of, 150–151; roles of, 18, 18n1, 20, 89–90, 102; success of, 3–4; synonyms for, 18; time of, 31–37; tips for, 12–15, 166–167
moderator-controlled discussion, 68–69
Moderator prestage, 168
moderator style development: audience engagement relating to, 150–151, 154; authenticity relating to, 149; empathy relating to, 149; focus relating to, 150; formal, 149; humor relating to, 149, 174; panelist summary relating to, 152–153; uniqueness relating to, 149
Moderator Time Calculator, 33–34, 40
multipurpose panel, 46

Nagaswami, Ranji, x, 25
networking, 38
nonprofit organizations, 82
nonverbal cues, 173
notecards, list, tablet, 71–73, 182
number: of panelists, 54–56; of questions, 102–104

objectives. *See* panel discussion objectives
objectivity, 19
O'Casey, Sean, 122
open-ended questions, 19, 111, 178
opening speeches, panelist introductions and: benefits of, 117–119; drafting of, 120; length of, 118–119, 120–121; practice of, 123; rehearsal of, 118, 122–123; Sample Opening Remarks, 121–122; statistics used with, 119
organizers. *See* advice, for organizers
Ostrander, Katie Flood: on engagement, 150; on panel organization, 53; on tightrope, 147

panel, 143–144; assemblage of, 32; boredom with, 65–66; checklist for, 10–12, 16, 160–161; close out of, 178–179; content for, 97, 99–100, 133–134; debates with, 18–19, 25; direction and flow of, 102–103; ending of, 175; evaluation of, 202; format of, 68–71; fun with, 153–154; goals of, 2–3, 17; how-to-guide for, 8–17; length of, 55; moderator and, 1–2; multipurpose, 46; preparation for, 133–134, 137; purpose of, 18, 34–35, 43–46, 126; relationships with, 4–7; as stuck, 169–170; templates for, 10–12, 16. *See also* panelist selection; panel topic choice; prepanel planning; *specific panel*

panel, types of: academic, 70; colloquy, 69–70; debate, 69; educational, 184; informational, 201; long *vs.* short panel, 76; sequential, 69

panel day, 163, 167–168; arrival, 162; dress for, 161; nerves during, 166; plan for, 159–160; start time, 164–165; timer for, 165

panel discussion objectives: continuing education, 45; fundraising and friend raising, 45–46; information, 44; membership building, 45; raising awareness, 44–45; sales, 44

panel hiccups: audience interrupter, 194–195; audience question issues, 197–198; audio issues, 190–191; creative solutions to, 191; disengaged audience, 196–197; distractions, 191–192; going off topic, 195; hidden agendas, 192–193; outside noise, 191–192; panelist interrupter, 193–194; question to wrong panelist, 192; reserved panelists, 195; ringing cell phones, 193; short answers, 196; technical difficulties, 190–191

panelist introductions. *See* opening speeches, panelist introductions and

panelist preparation calls, 81–82; group prep calls, 88–93; individual prepanel, 83–87, 124

Panelist Prestage, 167

panelists: benefits of, 117–119, 131–132; contact information of, 200; feedback from, 201; pointers for, 138–139; potential, 56–59; reiterating, 174; research on, 82; summary relating to, 152–153; title for, 89

panelists, type of: absent, 189–190; demanding, 64–65; extrovert, 81–82, 181; "friendly," 55–56; introvert, 81–82; long-winded, 172–174; reiterating, 174; scripted, 58; star, 158; unscripted, 58

panelist selection, 53; contributions relating, 58; diversity relating to, 62–63; experience relating to, 58; "friendly" panelist, 55–56; identification with, 56–59; number, 54–56; preselection relating to, 63–64; ranking

relating to, 58; "the ask" relating to, 59–62
panel marketing, 90, 95; advance audience polling, 98–99; creative ideas for, 97–98; participation relating to, 96–97; QR-driven content with, 99–100; title relating to, 94. *See also* Social Media and Event Promotion Guide
panel moved forward, 169–171
panel topic choice, 51, 144; brainstorming with, 43, 102; relevancy of, 42–43
photographer, 163
photos, on LinkedIn, 163
pivot trick, 140
planning. *See* prepanel planning
"plant," in audience, 181, 185–186
pointers, 138–140
polling: of audience, 49, 74–76, 98–99, 183–185, 197; technology for, 49, 74–76, 98–99
Postpanel, 205
postpanel marketing, 201–202
postpanel question time, 126, 199
potential panelists, 58–59
practice, of opening speeches and panelist introductions, 123
Preacceptance, 40
Preferred movie and television genres, *184*
prepanel day prep talk, 152–158; moderator presence, 150–151; moderator style relating to, 147–150; reminder list relating to, 147–148

prepanel planning, 183; audience understanding relating to, 47–51, 57; panel topic choice, 42–43; purpose of, 43–46; research with, 51–52; title, 46–47
prepanel polling, 185
preparation, 9–10, 32–34, 172; S. Brown on, 15; Carr on, 104; with how-to-guide, 15–17; for interviews, 22; Kaplowitz on, 104; for panel, 133–134, 137. *See also* panelist preparation calls; prepanel planning; questions, preparation of
prep calls. *See* specific prep calls
preselected panelists, 63–64
prestage: Moderator prestige, 168; Panelist Prestage, 167
profiles, in LinkedIn, 57
promotion, 89, 97
pronunciation, 157–158
protocol, with communication, 82
publications, 129
purpose: misalignment of, 34–35; of panel, 18, 34–35, 43–46, 126, 142; of prepanel planning, 43–46

Q&A. *See* question-and-answer session
QR. *See* quick-response code-driven content
question-and-answer (Q&A) session, 69, 126, 127, 170, 180, 185, 188
"question comfort zone," 84–85
questioner diversity, 186–187

questions, 2, 126, 192, 199; from audience, 176–177; Carr on, 101; digital question submission, 182–183; during individual prep call, 132–133; out of, 175–176; for stuck panel, 169–170. *See also* audience questions, handling of

questions, preparation of, 35–37, 129; allocation, 107, 113; development, 104–106; fun facts relating to, 114–115; number, 102–104; order relating to, 107–109; transitions relating to, 109–112; types of, 19, 84, 105–106, 110–114

questions, types of: crowdsourcing, 111–112; "gotcha," 113–114; open-ended, 19, 111, 178; "reactive," 181; tough, 136; worst, 187–188

Questions to Ask Before Accepting, 35–37, 40

Question Template, 115–116

quick-response (QR) code-driven content, 99–100

rabble-rousers, 194
ranking, with panelist selection, 58
rapport, with panel, 85
"reactive" questions, 181
read, of audience, 170
recording, 96, 98, 123, 200
rehearsal, of opening speeches and panelist introductions, 118, 122–123
reimbursement, 36, 86, 146
reiterating panelist, 174
relationships: building of, 200–201; career benefits of, 38, 39; with panel, 4–7

relevancy, of panel topic, 42–43
reminder list, 147–148
research time, 32, 34, 51–52, 82, 83
roles, of moderator, 20, 89–90, 102
"Rules of the Panel," 90–93

sales, 44
sales panel, 202
sample emails, 61–62
Sample Opening Remarks, 121–122
sample social media content, 97
scenario-based panel, 108–109
scripted panelists, 58
self-assurance, benefit of, 39
sequential panel, 69
session: facilitated session participant, 24; information for, 69, 129. *See also* question-and-answer session
skills: of changemakers, vii–xix, 2; leadership, 39
slide presentations, 74, 85–86
smartphone stopwatch, 165
social media, for panelist identification, 57
Social Media and Event Promotion Guide: follow Us on social media, 97; panel title, 96; promotional links, 96; promotional text, 96–97; sample social media content, 97; speaker promotional text, 97
Speaker Brief, 93, 127, 143, 189; biographies, 130; logistics information, 128; for panelists, 13–14; panel logistics, 124–125; panel purpose, 126; panel questions, 129; postpanel

question time, 126, 199; as prepanel marketing email, 89, 90; publications, 129; run of show, 125–126; session information, 69, 129
speaker promotional text, 97
speak slowly, 157
speeches. *See* opening speeches, panelist introductions and
Spiderman, 6
sponsoring organization, 56
spontaneity, 171–172
stage fright, 165
stage setup, 71–72
star panelist, 158
statistics, 119, 133nn1–2
Steel, Alix, 54, 147; on engagement, 164; on interaction, 20, 180; on nerves, 166
story-board panel, 68
storytelling, 134, 139, 154–156
strategies: for individual prepanel prep calls, 84–85; for timekeeper, 103–104, 110
structure and logistics, 67, 101–102; long *vs.* short panel, 76; notecards, list, tablet, 71–73; panel format, 68–71; stage setup, 71–72; technological considerations, 72–76; virtual panel, 77–80
success, of moderator, 3–4
summary, 152–153, 178
synonyms, for moderator, 18

technology, 19, 73, 161, 183; polling, 49, 74–76, 98–99, 145
TED Talks, 153, 155

Temerty Faculty Of Medicine, 30, 30n6
templates, 10–12, 16, 115–116
"Ten Tips for Moderating a Panel," 12
thank-you emails, 200
time: Horowitz on, 166; of moderator, 31–37; of panel, 175. *See also* Moderator Time Calculator
timekeeper strategies, 103–104, 110
tips, for moderator, 12–15, 166–167
"Tips for First Time Panelists," 12
title, for panel, 46–47, 89, 96, 157–158
Top Chef, 8–9, 170
topic, for panel. *See* panel topic choice
tough questions, tips for, 136
traits, of moderating, ix, 24–25
transitions, 109–112, 171
travel: reimbursement of, 146; time for, 32

Understanding the Audience, 47–51
unscripted panelists, 58

Valentine, Nicole, 3, 7, 148, 155
virtual panel, 77–80
visibility, benefit of, 38
vulnerabilities, 155–156

warmup poll, 183
winners, of panel, 177
wonder, in audience, 153–154
word cloud, 184
word poll, 184
worst questions, 187–188
writing, 22

GPSR Authorized Representative: Easy Access System Europe, Mustamäe tee 50, 10621 Tallinn, Estonia, gpsr.requests@easproject.com

www.ingramcontent.com/pod-product-compliance
Lightning Source LLC
Chambersburg PA
CBHW032337300426
44109CB00041B/1077